Cambridge Elements ≡

Elements in Global Development Studies
edited by
Peter Ho
Zhejiang University
Servaas Storm
Delft University of Technology

TEMPORARY MIGRANTS FROM SOUTHEAST ASIA IN AUSTRALIA

Lost Opportunities

Juliet Pietsch
Griffith University

CAMBRIDGE
UNIVERSITY PRESS

Shaftesbury Road, Cambridge CB2 8EA, United Kingdom

One Liberty Plaza, 20th Floor, New York, NY 10006, USA

477 Williamstown Road, Port Melbourne, VIC 3207, Australia

314–321, 3rd Floor, Plot 3, Splendor Forum, Jasola District Centre,
New Delhi – 110025, India

103 Penang Road, #05–06/07, Visioncrest Commercial, Singapore 238467

Cambridge University Press is part of Cambridge University Press & Assessment,
a department of the University of Cambridge.

We share the University's mission to contribute to society through the pursuit of
education, learning and research at the highest international levels of excellence.

www.cambridge.org
Information on this title: www.cambridge.org/9781009224208

DOI: 10.1017/9781009224215

First published 2022

A catalogue record for this publication is available from the British Library.

ISBN 978-1-009-22420-8 Paperback
ISSN 2634-0313 (online)
ISSN 2634-0305 (print)

Temporary Migrants from Southeast Asia in Australia

Lost Opportunities

Elements in Global Development Studies

DOI: 10.1017/9781009224215
First published online: September 2022

Juliet Pietsch
Griffith University
Author for correspondence: Juliet Pietsch, j.pietsch@griffith.edu.au

Abstract: Much of the scholarship in development studies focuses on developing countries. However, many of the same issues can be seen in developed countries, where migrants now constitute a sizeable proportion of the poor and politically disenfranchised. In immigrant-receiving countries such as Australia, temporary migrants in low-income households are most at risk of poor social and health outcomes. This research explores the experiences of temporary migrant workers from Southeast Asia in Australia, demonstrating that migrant workers, on the whole, live without a political voice or clear pathway to permanent residency and citizenship. The research is informed by Amartya Sen and Martha Nussbaum's theoretical framework of capabilities. One of the most critical capabilities is having a sense of political agency and control over one's environment. Given the significant increase in temporary migration flows around the world, this Element draws attention to the necessity of migrants to be provided with political capabilities.

Keywords: political capabilities, temporary migration, Southeast Asia, Australia, development

ISBNs: 9781009224208 (PB), 9781009224215 (OC)
ISSNs: 2634-0313 (online), 2634-0305 (print)

Contents

1 Introduction

The Covid-19 outbreak of late 2019, which became a global pandemic in 2020, has had a significant impact on the vulnerable and global poor in both developing and developed countries (Guadagno, 2020; Liu et al., 2021). The significant impact of pandemics on these groups, however, is not a recent phenomenon (see Davies, 2019). Before the onset of the pandemic, due to systematic inequalities in social determinants of health, those with poor social and health outcomes were consistently more vulnerable to disease (Kluge et al., 2020). While much of the scholarship in development studies focuses on developing countries, many of the same issues are transferred to developed countries where migrants from developing countries constitute a sizeable proportion of the poor and politically disenfranchised. In settler immigrant countries such as the United States, Canada, New Zealand and Australia, temporary migrants in low-income households are most at risk of poor social and health outcomes. In many cases, migrants, who on the whole live without a political voice or clear pathway to citizenship, find themselves living as denizens in third world conditions on the fringes of large urban cities or in isolated rural areas. The term 'denizen' is often used to refer to people who reside in a community without having the status of citizenship. Hammar (1990) originally used it to refer to settled immigrants who function in host societies almost indistinguishably from citizens but lack the formal citizenship that would give them full electoral rights. Baubock (2007) redefined it as 'a status of residential quasi-citizenship combined with external formal citizenship' (p. 2396). Many denizens have limited social and political rights, which translates to an inability to shape and influence policies and laws that may improve their circumstances. Instead, disempowered, they live in transit, in an indefinite liminal zone, subject to the neoliberal economic agenda that drives the decision making of global and domestic political institutions on migration.

The circumstances of Australia's disenfranchised migrants, trapped in social and political conditions with limited financial resources, were made clear at the onset of Melbourne's second wave of the Covid-19 pandemic in mid-2020. After struggling through the first wave with relatively little attention, on a grey mid-winter's Saturday afternoon, thousands of new migrants in the Flemington public housing towers in Melbourne's inner north were placed into a hard lockdown, with no warning. At the time, it was the most severe Covid-19 outbreak response witnessed in Australia, reminiscent of the restrictions of movement in Wuhan in China that so shocked the world earlier in the year. Thousands of vulnerable low-income tower residents, largely migrants, were not even allowed an opportunity to purchase essential food and medicine supplies. Parents or children who were elsewhere in the city were unable to return and visitors who happened to be at the apartments at the time were not allowed to leave. As the premier of Victoria was making the announcement on television, the apartment precinct was swarmed by hundreds of armed police, the darkening evening lit up by the flashing blue lights of dozens of police vehicles. As reported in the media, community leaders, the local government and the Department of Health and Human Services, which was responsible for administering the housing estate and the pandemic response, were also given no notice; the police officers themselves were only given the barest of warnings (Simons, 2020). There were no interpreters, no social workers and no medical staff in the first day or two of the operation, which was on a weekend. Upon media questioning, vague promises were given through the media that food and medicine would be delivered to residents who required it, 'as soon as possible'. Yet these deliveries were significantly delayed, until well into the following week. Neighbouring residents in nearby non-public houses and apartment buildings were unaffected and carried on their lives as normal.

Many of the residents of the locked down towers were from non-English-speaking backgrounds, with a significant proportion from war-torn and trauma-tised backgrounds. Even as the lockdown got underway, there was little to no consultation or deliberation with the residents about the logistics and potential health impacts. In halting English, residents and their families or community representatives located outside the apartments described the experience as deeply upsetting, and deeply traumatising. Even when food deliveries belatedly arrived, the food was thoughtlessly impractical or inedible, with deliveries of noodles, pasta or bacon and other pork products placed by masked police officers into the lobbies of the towers, which housed many Muslim migrants. The Victorian Ombudsman, Deborah Glass, later found that the lockdown was justified on public health grounds due to the rising number of Covid-19 cases emerging in the towers. However, the Ombudsman also found that the sudden implementation of the lockdown without warning was not justified and, in fact, caused fundamental breaches of human rights. The Ombudsman concluded the government had assumed the towers were 'a hotbed of criminality and non-compliance and that the people could not be trusted, if warning was given, not to escape the lockdown' (Victorian Ombusman, 2020). The Ombudsman was particularly critical of the attitudes underpinning the action: 'It is unimaginable that such stereotypical assumptions, leading to the "theatre of policing" that followed, would have accompanied the response to an outbreak of Covid-19 in a luxury apartment block' (Victorian Ombusman, 2020).

Demonstrating that this incident was not a random accident, almost a year later, due to an outbreak of the highly infectious Delta variant of Covid-19, residents of Sydney's western suburbs, largely comprising new migrants and the working class, were also treated harshly. For over a year, the New South Wales (NSW) state government had responded to numerous outbreaks without imposing any of the heavy restrictions used in other states. However, by late June 2021, with rising cases of community transmission, particularly in southwestern Sydney, which is highly populated with new migrants and older migrants from non-English-speaking and lower socio-economic backgrounds, a major police operation was launched targeting multicultural areas. The operation saw many hundreds of additional police officers patrolling the streets and malls of Liverpool, Fairfield and Canterbury-Bankstown local government areas. Mounted police were added as reinforcements to the initial blitz, to patrol the main shopping areas in the region. In the following weeks, at the request of the NSW government, hundreds of Australian Defence Force (ADF) soldiers were deployed to help the police combat residents flouting stay-at-home restrictions amid rising case numbers. This was despite concerns raised by multiple community leaders that for many migrants and refugees in Western Sydney, the sight of soldiers walking the streets had the potential to bring back the trauma of their war-torn countries of origin, where the military were often a direct source of threat and harm.

Over several months, hundreds – if not thousands – of fines were handed out for breaches of Covid-19 restrictions, often to residents who had simply not received or understood the public messaging. This high-density part of Sydney has a population of over a million people, where a higher proportion of residents do not speak English as their first language and do not usually receive their news from watching daily press conferences (Davey, 2021). The strong police response, supported by police horses, police dogs, and the aforementioned ADF soldiers, was heavily criticised, especially when compared to the 'soft touch' of other outbreak responses in Sydney's wealthy northern beaches and leafy eastern suburbs. The president of the Lebanese Muslim Association, Samir Dandan, for example, observed that the police had not cracked down as hard on other Sydney areas over the duration of the pandemic and the 'disproportionate' response in Sydney's west would be harmful to the largely migrant community (Kontominas & Taouk, 2021).

As Sydney's lockdown dragged on for months afterwards, the divide between western Sydney and the rest of the city only worsened. This divide was at its most stark when, on the first weekend of spring, thousands of residents from Sydney's affluent east flocked to beaches to sunbake and swim – many without the mandatory face-masks, with only token efforts at social distancing – while the largely multicultural communities of Sydney's west were subject to harsh stay at home orders. In the words of Canterbury-Bankstown mayor Khal

Asfour, 'we saw the pictures of Bondi and Coogee and the eastern suburbs beaches, and I don't begrudge anyone that lives close to the beach to be able to go there, but when we're stuck at home and didn't have any hours of recreation, it makes my community angry, frustrated' (Butterworth, 2021). Exacerbating the situation, while thousands sun-baked and surfed on beaches without penalty, large numbers of police officers, as well as the riot squad, responded to reports that between 80 and 100 people were attending a funeral in Sydney's west, in breach of public health orders, resulting in arrests and fines. Politicians at all levels spoke out about the perceived injustice. Federal Labor MP Linda Burney, whose seat of Barton covers many of the local government areas of concern in western Sydney, said, 'I'm hearing from people … there is an absolute feeling of two cities … One where you see people going to the beach. And [another] where you've got helicopters flying over you with loudspeakers' (Butterworth, 2021).

There can be no argument that these experiences of injustice, disempowerment and human rights violations are common in developing countries. The severe lockdown of Wuhan, for instance, was generally understood to be part and parcel of China's hard, yet effective, Covid-19 response. Evidently, third world or developing countries, or even countries under authoritarian rule such as China, do not have a monopoly on such incidents. As described by an anonymous government official involved in the front line of Melbourne's tower block lockdown, 'In February I watched television showing the Chinese police nailing up apartment doors in Wuhan and welding people into their buildings to stop the spread of Covid-19. I thought we would never do anything like that here. Then a few months later, I was part of doing pretty much exactly the same. It made me question everything I had given my life to' (Simons, 2021). Unfortunately, as this incident reveals, disempowerment, coupled with breaches of human rights, can occur for migrants from poor backgrounds in any country, including developed countries such as Australia.

Temporary migrants, largely from underprivileged backgrounds, face an array of barriers, many of them insurmountable, in not only asserting their social and political rights in times of crisis but also in advocating for longer-term policy change that may improve social and health outcomes in their communities. While some may have rights potentially allowing them to forge a pathway to citizenship, they are not always able to act on those rights. They face multiple structural barriers associated with gender, class, race and ethnicity, resulting in widespread inequality. These migrants, who are often living in third-world-like conditions, require more attention in development studies scholarship. Equally, they need to play a more meaningful role in the United Nation's 2030 Agenda for Sustainable Development. For many of these migrants, everyday life bears little resemblance to the opportunities and rights of citizens. Often vulnerable to homelessness, ill-health and violence, the status of being temporary and on a low income produces a wide range of social, health and community concerns. The situation is steadily worsening, with sharp increases in violence and ill-feelings towards migrants from disadvantaged backgrounds across contexts and nations, and with a tightening of pathways to citizenship. Moreover, developed countries are both economically dependent on, and seemingly intent on delimiting, the migrant as a social, political and civic actor. This decay in the migrant's status and opportunities across societies is palpable, yet rarely systematically examined within the development studies field.

This element will delineate the state of the temporary migrant and their political rights in Australia, providing the evidence-base needed to enliven policy and practical efforts to prevent the erosion of civic participation and political representation through a unique comparative analysis. The research is informed by Amartya Sen and Martha Nussbaum's theoretical framework of capabilities (Sen 2002, 2005; Nussbaum, 2011). It draws attention to the necessity of migrants to be provided with political rights, and a degree of freedom and agency so that they are not victims of the types of experiences felt by the public housing tenants preceding the city of Melbourne's second wave lockdown, that left them feeling so traumatised by the state. As an interdisciplinary political sociologist, I also aim to generate a constructive interdisciplinary discussion between political science and development studies.

The overall migration–development nexus reveals a predominance of neoliberal approaches of governments in sending and receiving countries and their tendency to focus on the economic benefits of migration at the cost of political rights that will enhance individual freedom, well-being and agency. According to Carney (2007), this injection of neoliberal values has transformed and degraded the coverage of the welfare state. Carney argues that this has marked an abandonment of the acceptance of state responsibility for the victims of economic and social restructuring, or of any serious commitments towards building the contested notion of 'social capital'. One consequence is that the individual migrant, rather than the state, is expected to assume greater responsibility for managing future adverse contingencies within the global political economy.

According to Sen and Williams (1982), such neoliberal arrangements between governments have failed to prioritise rights, freedoms and human agency. Consequently, some approaches to human development have similarly and implicitly accepted a neoliberal development paradigm (Saith, 2006). For example, Saith (2006) argues that both the human development approach and

the related Millennium and Sustainable Development Goals have limited their
policy alternatives to interventions that are compatible with the neoliberal
policy template. With an overemphasis on the social and economic aspects of
migration, the migration–development approach underestimates the signifi-
cance of political rights in the achievement of individual freedom, well-being
and agency. Therefore, there is a need to explore the complexity of the migration–development nexus, the 'capabilities approach' to development studies
and the need to bolster the importance of political rights and representation, as
a means to achieving freedom, well-being and agency. Migrants from low-
income backgrounds without a political voice or a pathway to citizenship are
more likely to suffer from poor social and health impacts – that are often
commensurate with third world conditions – compared to those with political
representation and/or citizenship.

The 2020 UNDP report highlights the various types of inequalities that exist
within countries such as Australia which, has deep roots in colonialism and
racism (UNDP, 2020). These inequalities, and their historic roots, limit the
potential of future positive social and political outcomes for new migrants,
minimising their ability to meaningfully contribute, let alone affect change. In
the same report, there is recognition of the need for a new generation of human
development metrics that add planetary environmental pressures to the existing
measures of income, health, education, inequality, gender and poverty (UNDP,
2020, p. 227). Within the context of escalating planetary pressures, the multiple
voices of climate-exposed temporary migrants need to be included in national
and international climate change political debates as agents with a long history
of displacement and population mobility (Farbotko & Lazrus, 2012). Yet,
without a political voice, their experiences are often silenced in favour of the
more immediate needs of the local political economy. While the UN has
determined that climate change temporary migrants should not be returned
home, it is unlikely that governments in receiving countries will accept climate
refugees as permanent migrants with a pathway to citizenship.

To explore these broad issues in more detail, taking Australia as an exemplar
of a dynamic that has unfolded across immigrant-receiving polities, I explain
how government policies have helped to generate a politically disempowered
underclass that has, ironically, helped form the nation's economic backbone.
I first begin with a background of the political economic context underpinning
temporary migration and its impact on migrants from developed countries such
as Australia. In the second section I look at the migration–development nexus in
settler societies and how the 'capabilities approach' developed by Sen and
Nussbaum, with its strengths and limitations, provides a useful framework for
understanding the migration–development nexus and the issues that face

migrants from developing countries. While the UNDP human development reports emphasise several positive economic impacts for both origin and destination countries, what is often missing in these economic accounts of development and migration are the individual political experiences of migrants themselves, many of whom have limited or no pathways to citizenship.

In the final section, I draw on qualitative interviews and focus group discussions with migrant actors from Southeast Asia. In Australia, a significant proportion of poor migrants are from Southeast Asia and are, collectively, more likely to face social and political discrimination because of their race, ethnicity or religion (Pietsch, 2018). On the whole, they have migrated to Australia either as students or through temporary worker programs (Hugo et al., 2015). Many temporary migrants often work in low-paid insecure jobs, are income poor and struggle to access permanent residency or citizenship pathways. In addition, they can be locked out of the social and political benefits of capital gains, capital income and intergenerational transfers that are pre-eminent among the established political class and a major cause of growing inequality (Adkins et al., 2019).

2 The Migration–Development Nexus

Temporary migration schemes are generally supported and promoted by governments as a way of addressing short-term economic gaps in the labour market in the country of destination, and by contributing substantially to remittances in the country of origin. The scholarship on the topic consistently refers to labour migration as a 'win-win' solution or, if the process involves repeat or circular temporary migration, a 'triple win' solution:

> It offers destination countries a steady supply of needed workers in both skilled and unskilled occupations, without the requirements of long-term integration. Countries of origin can benefit from the inflow of remittances while migrants are abroad and skills upon return. The migrants are also thought to gain much, as the expansion of circular migration programs increases the opportunities for safer, legal migration from the developing world (Agunias & Newland, 2007, p. 1).

In pursuit of at least the first two wins of the so-called triple win, temporary migration programs often involve a great deal of collaboration between origin and destination countries (Plewa, 2007). For instance, the development-oriented migration policies supported by the International Organization of Migration (IOM) are frequently designed in a way to address the economic needs of both countries of origin and destination countries. Wages stemming from migrant labour in destination countries, and the subsequent transfer of private funds or remittances to enhance the development of countries of origin, are a key feature of the migration–development nexus. While the IOM recognises the link between migration and economic, social and cultural development, as well as the right of freedom of movement, the absence of political rights in the country of final destination means that migrants have little agency in improving their own conditions, albeit with some ability, through remittances, to enhance development in their countries of origin. In other words, migrants are forced to 'trade off' their own human rights for the social and economic development priorities of their countries of origin and destination.

In development studies there have been attempts to address the human rights violations and worsening conditions of temporary migrants in developed countries. For instance, there have been many reports released by national and multilateral organisations which focus on the benefits of the linkages between migration and development (OECD, 2019; IOM, 2020; ILO, 2021). However, the most well-known attempts to build collaboration and compliance in countries have been the Millennium Development Goals (MDGs) and the SDGs. In terms of the MDGs, there were over eighteen targets and forty-eight indicators specified in the MDG template. However, the MDGs located development in the third world, even though, as discussed earlier, there is significant poverty and deprivation experienced by temporary migrants in advanced economies.

In reference to the MDGs, Saith (2006) argues that the human development approach taken by the MDGs had limited its policy recommendations to those that fall within the neoliberal development agenda. Migration, for example, was viewed as critical for economic growth and poverty alleviation, but there was little focus in the MDG agenda on migrant rights. Moreover, while the words 'participation', 'empowerment' and 'poverty reduction' often gain considerable purchase in the language of mainstream development, few migrants from temporary migrant backgrounds have had opportunities to participate meaningfully in political institutions where their voices can be heard on the policies that impact their day-to-day lives (Cornwell & Brock, 2005). This is reflected in the global response to the SDGs, adopted by the United Nations in 2015, which, is focused on documenting national or state activities or processes, with a cursory nod to non-governmental or, in the case of the migrant experience, community input. As the SDGs pivot to addressing the Covid-19 pandemic, there is a real need to re-examine the existing development theories and policies to include political rights, membership and belonging. Such a call for action is not new (see, for example, Preibisch et al., 2016), but has gained greater salience now that the UN has been more focussed on the global pandemic response.

The capacity for new and vulnerable migrants to participate in host-country politics differ markedly in western countries, with some countries depriving non-citizens of any formal means of political participation (IDEA, 2018). The means to participation depends heavily on citizenship and electoral laws in each country. There are more than forty-five countries which give voting rights to non-citizens, especially at the local level (Pedroza, 2014; Ernest, 2015). While a very small number of countries allow non-citizens to vote in national elections – namely New Zealand, Malawi and Uruguay – most only permit voting in elections for local, state or regional elections such as EU parliamentary elections (Ernest, 2015, p. 863). This is despite the United Nations Human Rights Council's assertion that 'effective participation in decision-making processes, particularly those which have an impact on minorities, is a precondition for the full and equal enjoyment of the human rights of persons belonging to minorities' (UNHRC, 2010, p. 2). They argue that 'the denial of citizenship has been used by states to exclude minorities from the enjoyment of their rights' and therefore governments should 'consider allowing non-citizens belonging to minorities to vote, stand as candidates in local elections, and be members of the governing boards of self-governing bodies, while making sure that access to citizenship is regulated in a non-discriminatory manner' (UNHRC, 2010, p. 16).

New Zealand is a notable case study by international standards for their liberal and inclusive system of electoral rights, whereby those who are defined as non-citizen 'permanent residents' and who have lived in New Zealand for at least a year can vote in national elections under Section 73 of the Electoral Act 1993 (Barker & McMillan, 2016, p. 7). The other significant feature of New Zealand's franchise laws are the seven separate seats for Māori to ensure adequate political representation in national elections (Barker & McMillan, 2016, p. 13). However, like Australia, New Zealand is experiencing an increase in the number of temporary migrants who are not offered a pathway to permanent residency and citizenship.

Even though non-citizens may not be able to vote across all levels of government, there are often opportunities to participate in non-formal forms of political participation such as advocating on an issue in their host country, participating in peaceful protests on certain policies or actively participating on social media by commenting on or sharing political ideas. However, these opportunities are often constrained by poverty, restrictions on mobility, weak institutional protections, fear of losing one's visa or experiences of discrimination and racism. Cumulatively, these concerns block or hamstring access to political representatives and established networks. Furthermore, according to Pedroza (2014), non-citizen or 'denizen' enfranchisement matters because 'voting is the only universal form of political participation that, independently of the formulae to aggregate votes, recognizes an equal voice for each person in the *demos*' (p. 26). While some may choose not to vote in countries without compulsory voting, the right to vote is crucial as for migrants, it 'implies recognition as equals in the political community' (Pedroza, 2014, p. 26). This also safeguards non-voters of vulnerable stigmatised groups such as asylum seekers – often denied basic human rights – from being the object of political campaigns, instead of the clientele (Pedroza, 2014, p. 26). The overall circumstances of temporary migrants are often far from positive, especially since there has been a remarkable convergence in policymaking in wealthier destination countries in the region which have significantly escalated border security and surveillance, while also experiencing an increasing demand for cheap labour with limited protections.

Australia provides a good case study to examine the impact of the increasing denial of long-term pathways towards permanent residency and political rights in a developed country. Since 2011, temporary migrants have comprised the bulk of migrant flows to Australia (Boucher & Gest, 2018). Temporary migrants in Australia make up the majority of overseas arrivals in Australia (62.1 per cent) (ABS, 2021). Until the mid-1990s Australia's immigration policy focused almost exclusively on permanent settlement as opposed to temporary migration. However, this changed dramatically with the introduction in 1996 of a skilled temporary worker visa (Subclass 457). In 2018, the Australian Government replaced the 457 visas with Temporary Skills Shortage (TSS) visas (Subclass 482). Applicants are required to have two years with relevant work experience, be proficient in English and remain in the same job. Employers can also sponsor workers on the TSS visa through a labour agreement involving the federal government.

Skilled temporary migrants are ranked under categories which prioritise those who have occupational skills on the Priority Migration Skilled Occupation List (PMSOL). All other applicants on temporary visas are placed at the bottom of the list and can wait for years for an outcome, even though they may meet the requirements of permanent residency. For instance, family applicants are placed in a queue and may have to wait for years before they reach the front of the queue, with many applicants waiting more than ten years (Australian Department of Home Affairs, 2022). Many temporary migrants do not leave Australia when their visas expire. Instead, they tend to transfer to another visa type while they wait in the queue for an outcome on their permanent residency application (Mares, 2012). Many temporary migrants wait in limbo or move to regional areas with the hope of being able to transition to a permanent visa after three to five years. One avenue has been through the Regional Sponsored Migration Scheme Subclass 187

(RSMS) visa (since replaced by the Subclass 494 visa) which allows temporary migrants to become permanent residents after they live and work in regional Australia for several years. While these visas may offer permanent residency, findings show that employers are sponsoring a growing number of low-wage workers with few skills, at risk of exploitation (Coates et al., 2022).

Other temporary visas include those for international students, working holiday makers and Special Category Visas (SPV) for New Zealanders (Subclass 444). International students are allowed to work for twenty hours a week during their studies and contribute to the low-skilled casualised workforce. Working Holiday visas allow temporary migrants to live in Australia for twelve months. Temporary migrants on Working Holiday visas primarily come from other developed countries such as the UK, Germany, France, Ireland, Taiwan, South Korea and Japan. They have been highly sought after because they tend to spend more money in the local economy compared to temporary labour migrants (Mares, 2012).

In 2009, Australia introduced the Seasonal Worker Program (SWP), with the Pacific Labour Scheme (PLS) introduced in 2018. These two programs were merged into the Pacific Australia Labour Mobility (PALM) Scheme which involves recruiting workers from up to ten Pacific countries to migrate to Australia for up to three years. Pacific Islanders can also migrate to Australia via New Zealand after becoming permanent residents or citizens of New Zealand through the Trans-Tasman Travel Arrangement, often referred to as step-migration (Vasta, 2004). The Trans-Tasman Arrangement is essentially a policy which treats New Zealanders as temporary migrants for the purposes of welfare assistance and citizenship. However, they differ from other temporary migrants because they can reside indefinitely in Australia, and they are not entitled to any form of disability assistance. McMillan (2017) highlights the unique case of New Zealanders in Australia who often have the right to indefinite residency but not welfare assistance or citizenship acquisition following changes to the relevant Australian legislation in 2001. McMillan's research finds that migrants under this scheme described strong feelings of exclusion, rejection, exploitation and discrimination (McMillan, 2017, p. 115). Except for the SPVs for New Zealanders, most temporary visa programs tend to have limited options for permanent residency, creating a 'trapdoor' by channelling workers into a permanent temporary status with no pathways to permanent residency (Howe et al., 2019, p. 220). In general, the TSS visas have involved limiting the pathways to permanent residency compared to the previous 457 visas and an expansion of labour market testing requirements to protect Australian workers.

There have been growing reports of exploitation and abuse within Australia's temporary migration programs (Cibborn & Wright, 2018). Forms of exploitation include wage theft involving underpayment through wages, unlawful deductions and cash-back schemes, with more than half of Australia's temporary migrants paid less than the minimum wage (Stringer & Michailova, 2019, p. 5). The drivers of exploitation relate to the structural power relations that stem from being able to sponsor a temporary migrant, in their capacity as an employer, a partner or as an extended family member. This creates a system of bondage whereby temporary migrants often do not report their experiences of exploitation at the hands of an employer, partner or family member because of a fear of being deported, or a lack of knowledge or trust in the social, political and legal institutions that protect migrants in vulnerable circumstances. These vulnerabilities might well be known by their sponsor and exploited.

In 2020–2021, the exploitative conditions of temporary migration were made public when temporary migrants were among five Uber drivers who died in Australia while working without proper safety conditions (Thompson, 2022). However, because they were temporary migrant contractors working in the gig economy, the urgency for big corporations as well as state and federal governments to either improve conditions or take responsibility was met with a deafening silence. Most Uber drivers and other gig economy workers are students on temporary student visas. According to Ramia et al. (2021), policy inaction involving the neglect of the welfare needs of students, such as poor housing, homelessness and widespread job losses during the pandemic showed an example of calculated and ideological inaction. International students were essentially viewed as market subjects, whereas citizens were treated as welfare subjects (Ramia et al., 2021). The threat of labour market competition and the perception of migrants as a burden on the welfare system are significant factors underpinning the deterioration of migrant labour market and welfare conditions (Scheve & Slaughter, 2001; Facchini & Mayda, 2006; Dustmann & Preston, 2007).

The quality of life for temporary migrants without permanent residency or citizenship is further compromised by government practices which frequently involve the exploitation of temporary migrant labour. As mentioned, while temporary migrants are significant contributors to the labour market they are, at the same time, excluded from cultural and political belonging. In traditional settler countries such as Australia, governments and politicians tend to maximise utility by weighing up the costs and benefits of different categories of immigration in terms of the national interest. In fact, government legislative and policy frameworks are specifically designed to prevent pathways to permanent migration, hindering or hamstringing the future capacity of temporary migrants

to participate in society as active and engaged citizens capable of meaningfully addressing the problems they face.

In Australia, temporary migrants can be deported back to their country of
origin once their employment visa expires. Of course, it is the deportability
or 'easy-come, easy-go' nature of temporary migrants that makes them
attractive to potential employers, particularly in the domestic, agriculture,
horticulture and construction sectors. The high dependence on employers
means that temporary migrants will often accept worse conditions than the
local populations with permanent residency or citizenship. This may include
lower wages and few employment benefits such as medical or maternity or
paternity leave, as well as little say over their working hours (Preibisch et al.,
2016, p. 9). These conditions and the need to maintain ties with one's
employer often restrict the mobility of migrants and their capacity as agents
of development to seek advice on their social and political rights.
Furthermore, temporary migrants are often geographically isolated which,
in combination with limited public or private transport options, restricts their
mobility.

For migrants, extended family members are often critical for childcare
needs and extended family support. However, in Australia, grandparents are
now required to wait more than seventy months for their visas to be processed
(Boucher & Pacquet, 2021). Other costs associated with the lack of access to
full healthcare, education and public housing are also a significant burden for
temporary migrants. Migrants are not often able to advocate on behalf of their
communities about their limited rights in the workplace and associated problems with schooling and childcare, while they have a precarious visa status,
a lack of citizenship and franchise rights (Boucher & Pacquet, 2021). The
cumulative impact of these vulnerabilities means that temporary migrants
have limited financial, social and political capital to speak up about their
rights and participate in the policymaking process where positive change
could make a difference, not only to their own lives but also to those of their
communities.

3 Incorporating a Political Rights Framework

In order to provide migrants with a greater chance of affective integration with
a sense of 'belonging, recognition, equality, optimism and loyalty in, or to,
their country of residence' (see McMillan, 2017, p. 103), temporary migrants
should be both enfranchised as non-citizen residents and given a pathway to
citizenship and the political rights associated with it. Ensuring that migrants are
on a path to permanent residency also ensures that they are on a path to political

inclusion and political representation. This is because, in Australia, voting rights come with citizenship. Politicians will also be incentivised to better respond to the interests and experiences of new migrants who will, in time, be able to vote. Otherwise, as argued by Isin (2002), citizenship will continue to be an identity and practice through which political privilege and marginalisation are constructed. For Isin, the alien 'other' on the one hand and the citizen, on the other, are mutually constitutive. The insider identity is possible only through the marking of the outsider. Antje Missbach, a permanent resident in Australia who applied for citizenship twice and on both occasions her application was rejected, argues that 'citizenship is the very basis to claim rights, ergo not holding citizenship in the place where one happens to live is a powerful means of exclusion' (Missbach, 2018, p. 40).

Citizenship does not necessarily imply formal membership of a nation state but, rather, a position of inclusion in a political community. According to Isin (2002, p. 280), citizenship is the result of processes whereby 'certain groups . . . [constitute] . . . themselves as capable of being political, in the sense of being endowed with the capacity to be governed by and govern other citizens and being differentiated from strangers and outsiders'. I argue that while enfranchising temporary migrants may not always be politically viable at the national level, an inclusive pathway that provides temporary migrants with the freedom to move, to choose their employer, to be employed under the same labour laws and regulations as citizens, and to have a basic level of welfare assistance that is inclusive of those with disabilities is necessary. The provision of these extra institutional protections will allow temporary migrants to have a sense of agency and belonging in their communities, and a chance to build a future where temporary migrants can participate from a position of inclusion in a political community. This would provide an informal inclusive social citizenship that is similar to Isin's conceptualisation of citizenship in terms of political inclusion and participation as a basic human right where migrants are entitled to meaningful participation in civil, political, economic, social and cultural development (Isin, 2002).

There are many benefits of linking the human rights of participation and social inclusion with development approaches (Preibisch et al., 2016, p. 12). Amartya Sen's theory of capabilities offers a fresh paradigm for analysing the political and social inclusion of migrants within developed countries. The most well-known of Sen's books, *Development as Freedom* (1999), uses the capability approach as a key element of what can be considered as an alternative vision on development. Sen's theory looks at what people are capable of doing and then, in turn, their ability to realise these capabilities (what they are 'free' or 'able' to choose to do). This is quite different from conventional measures which focus on a person's socio-economic or political resources. Robeyns best describes the capabilities approach as:

> the effective opportunities that people have to lead the lives they have reason to value. The core concepts in the capability approach are a person's functionings, which are her beings and doings (for example, being well-fed or literate), and her capabilities (the genuine opportunities or freedoms to realize these functionings) (Robeyns, 2006, p. 351).

One of the capabilities approach's major benefits is that it views people as individuals rather than in terms of their economic value or level of competitiveness in the labour market. The capabilities approach has made a foundational contribution to the growth of the human development paradigm, which is now well known, especially in light of the UNDP human development reports. There are a wide variety of capabilities that range from essential ones, such as being well nourished, to more complex ones, such as having self-respect and being free to participate in society. Of key importance are the ideas of freedom of choice and agency. While there is much discussion on the importance of social and political citizenship as a means to improving equality, true equality requires differential support depending on individual circumstances. For example, equality for migrants may be viewed not only in terms of economic indicators but also in terms of achieving sufficient esteem, recognition and self-respect in the workforce and within political institutions. As mentioned previously, the notable case of New Zealand and their more liberal system of electoral rights at the national level show at least on a symbolic level that New Zealand is committed to expanding their political community to include non-citizen permanent residents, which inevitably leads to a greater visibility of the concerns that they might face at the national level in parliamentary debates. The dedicated seats in parliament for Māori candidates also demonstrate a commitment to ensure that there is a diversity of voices heard in significant policymaking decisions that may disproportionately impact Māori populations living with more vulnerabilities and dependence on the nation state.

Restrictive immigration and integration policies can also impact the capacity for migrants to reach their full capabilities. In comparing Australia with other immigrant societies and several European immigrant-receiving countries, it is useful to look at the findings from the Migration Integration Policy Index (MIPEX). The MIPEX compares countries and looks at what governments are doing to promote integration and opportunities to participate meaningfully in society and improve standards for equal treatment (Migration Policy Group, 2021). The policy areas of integration covered by the MIPEX include labour market mobility, family reunification, education, political participation, permanent residence, access to nationality, anti-discrimination and health. The policy indicators in Table 1 are questions relating to a specific policy component. As can be seen, Australia lags behind New Zealand, the United States and Canada on offering permanent residence and pathways to nationality and citizenship.

While most countries have improved their policies on integration in the past five years, Australia has worsened (–4 points in the average MIPEX score), primarily because of the obstacles in labour market participation and the path to permanent residency. This is because most temporary migrants are not entitled to permanent residency until they have lived in Australia for more than five years. The path to permanent residency has been lengthened and restricted to fewer categories of temporary migration, especially within the skilled, family and refugee migration streams.

Even though the Australian government can improve the conditions for newcomers in granting equal rights, opportunities and a pathway to citizenship, capabilities do not always rely on the nation state but, due to structural barriers and discrimination, temporary migrants may need government assistance to provide the resources necessary to realise these capabilities (Briones, 2011; de Haas, 2012). For instance, differences in gender, class and ethnicity can hinder one's ability to achieve a sense of agency (Pfister, 2012, p. 248). Migrants living in poverty and with visas tied to an employer, for instance, may have human rights but not the capacity and the freedom to act on those rights because of other social or cultural constraints or power imbalances. Furthermore, while political institutions may set aside special seats in parliament or extend voting rights to non-citizens, this does not necessarily remove the social and political barriers to recognition, self-respect, equality and representation. For example, the barriers of discrimination and racial prejudice, as well as general concerns about migrants and their sense of loyalty to the nation state, are likely to constrain efforts to liberalise the political system and achieve the necessary foundational blocks needed for migrants to realise their full capabilities.

Therefore, it is important to look not only at inequality in terms of opportunities within a human rights framework but also at inequality in terms of actual outcomes (Sayer, 2012, p. 587). While some migrants from disadvantaged backgrounds – for example, new refugees or ethnic minorities – can participate in politics due to their citizenship status, in terms of outcomes, there are few who have had real opportunities to actively participate in politics in informal and formal networks because of their limited social, cultural and political capital. According to Sayer, the inequality of political outcomes can lead to a qualitative form of contributive injustice (Sayer, 2012, p. 586).

Table 1 Migration Integration Policy Index (MIPEX) Indicators, 2019.

	Overall Score	Political Participation	Permanent Residence	Access to Nationality	Anti-discrimination	Secure Future
Australia	65	65	46	76	69	64
NZ	77	85	63	92	88	82
US	73	40	63	88	97	67
Canada	80	50	77	88	100	72
UK	56	45	58	61	94	30
Sweden	86	80	90	83	100	86
Norway	69	80	71	50	65	57
Finland	85	95	96	74	100	78
Portugal	81	80	71	86	100	82
Ireland	64	85	50	79	94	57

Source: Migration Integration Policy Index, https://www.mipex.eu/what-is-mipex

Nussbaum's (2011) ten 'central human capabilities' – life; bodily health; bodily integrity; senses, imagination and thought; emotions; practical reason; affiliation; other species; play and control over one's environment – can have a significant influence on political outcomes. One of the most critical capabilities is having a sense of political agency and control over one's environment. Among other capabilities, Nussbaum argues the importance of 'being able to participate effectively in political choices that govern one's life; having the right of political participation, protections of free speech and association; having the right to seek employment on an equal basis with others; and being able to work as a human being, exercising practical reason and entering into meaningful relationships of mutual recognition with other workers' (Nussbaum, 2011, p. 33). As indicated previously, most temporary migrants are not able to achieve one or more of these types of capabilities within the context of the neoliberal economy. Therefore, the capabilities approach offers an alternative theoretical framework to reflect on the migration–development nexus and the need to incorporate greater attention to political rights and freedoms.

Overall, the capabilities approach is concerned with entrenched social injustice and inequality and suggests an urgent task for governments is to improve the quality of life for all people, as defined by their capabilities (Nussbaum, 2011, p. 19). It is, in Sen's words, 'an intellectual discipline that gives a central role to the evaluation of a person's achievements and freedoms in terms of his or her actual ability to do the different things a person has reason to value doing or being' (Sen, 2009, p. 16). In the following section I draw on human rights and capabilities approaches both used in development studies with qualitative research to identify the social and political struggles of temporary migrants to Australia from the Southeast Asian region. I focus on the way they interact with social and political institutions and feel a sense of belonging within the political community.

4 Southeast Asian Migrants in Australia

Australia has a long history of migration from Southeast Asia. While the numbers of Southeast Asian migrants in Australia started to increase during the post-war period, it was not until during the mid-to-late 1980s when the numbers began to increase as a proportion of the total migrant population, reaching a peak in 2006 of 12.5 per cent of all first-generation migrants in Australia (see Table 2).

Following the first significant wave of Southeast Asian migrants in Australia in the 1980s, most migrants arrived through family reunion migration schemes. Many were unskilled with low qualifications, settled in the outskirts of

Table 2 Southeast migrants in Australia, 1900–2016

	Southeast Asian Migrants (n)	Total Migrants (n)	Southeast Asian migrants (%)
1901	983	852,373	0.12
1911	462	752,627	0.06
1921	1,438	835,698	0.17
1933	2,564	901,071	0.28
1947	5, 391	742,896	0.73
1954	7,254	1,285,798	0.56
1961	15,371	1,777,849	0.86
1966	34,087	2,130,043	1.60
1971	75,322	2,578,538	2.92
1976	54,566	2,689,155	2.03
1981	132,118	2,950,857	4.48
1986	236,140	3,195,778	7.39
1991	374,211	3,684,969	10.16
1996	456,460	3,901,439	11.70
2001	487,475	4,063,759	12.00
2006	552,582	4,405,217	12.54
2011	701,865	5,280,441	13.29
2016	872,891	7,787,057	11.21

Source: Australian Bureau of Statistics, Census of Population and Housing, 1901–2016.

Australia's major cities and required significant support from the government in terms of assistance with English language skills and welfare (Jupp, 1995). With the rise in Asian immigration, critics argued that the government was moving too far ahead of public opinion. For example, historian Geoffrey Blainey argued that immigration policy in the early 1980s was insensitive to the views of the majority of the Australian population. In *All for Australia*, Blainey criticised Australia's multiculturalism policies and, in particular, the emergence of the government rhetoric that Australia is 'part of Asia' (Blainey, 1984). The criticisms of Blainey were later echoed in the mid-1990s when public opinion showed that there was some hesitation and anxiety surrounding the notion of a closer engagement with Asia (McAllister & Ravenhill, 1998). Overall, survey findings showed that support among the broader Australian public for multiculturalism rapidly declined during the 1990s (AES, 1993, 1996).

In line with public opinion, and pressure to address short-term skill shortages in the economy, by the mid-1990s Australia shifted its emphasis on family reunification migration programs towards skilled temporary migration.

Australia has since become heavily dependent on temporary skilled migration from Asia, with a significant proportion of temporary migrants now arriving from Southeast Asia. The barriers to citizenship also increased during this time period. In 2007, new requirements meant that applicants had to demonstrate integration into the community and pass a citizenship test. There was also an extension of the minimum permanent residency period from twelve months to four years. During this time, the visa extension application and citizenship test costs were significantly increased, making it more difficult for migrants to be able to afford to stay in Australia. These barriers and costs have since further increased, making it harder for migrants to qualify for permanent residency when they first arrive in Australia. Instead, many Southeast Asian migrants arriving on temporary visas hope to gain enough local education and employment experience in the right areas to qualify for permanent residency. At each stage of the process, there are significant financial and social costs that reduce people's capacity or their ability to realise their full capabilities.

In 2016 up to 37 per cent of migrants living in Australia did not have citizenship. Figure 1 shows that over the last few decades there has been a significant increase in the proportion of Southeast Asian migrants living in Australia without citizenship. In the early 1900s, more than 94 per cent of migrants from Southeast Asia had citizenship. This pattern continued until 1996 when the trend towards granting migrants citizenship declined rapidly to only 31 per cent of arrivals since 2006 granted citizenship. In Australia, migrants are required to live in Australia as a permanent resident for four years before they can apply for citizenship.

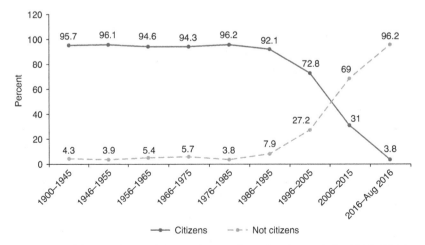

Figure 1 Citizen and non-citizen migrants from Southeast Asia, 1900–2016.
Source: 2016 Census, Australian Bureau of Statistics.

Table 3 Visa characteristics of migrants born in Southeast Asia, arrived in Australia, 2010–2019

Type of visa at November 2019	(n)
Australian citizen	63,100
Permanent visa	94,900
Skilled	40,900
Family	49,100
Humanitarian	8,100
Temporary visa	124,900
Total	298,600

Source: Australian Bureau of Statistics, Characteristics of Recent Migrants, Australia, 2019 Characteristics of Recent Migrants, Australia. Canberra: Australian Government.

While Australia can boast a rich immigration history, with its welcoming of migrants from Southeast Asia since the mid-1980s, as mentioned, it has been gradually closing its doors to permanent residency and citizenship for migrants from the region. Among recent arrivals from Southeast Asia (i.e. those who have arrived since 2011), the largest group of visa holders are temporary visa holders (124,900), followed by permanent resident visa holders (95, 900) and those who have arrived as Australian citizens (63,100).

The research shows that the 124,900 temporary visa holders are more likely to be exposed to greater risks of exploitation, insecurity and vulnerability than those who arrive as Australian citizens or on permanent visas (Coates et al., 2022). Australia now has limited long-term legal pathways to permanent residency and citizenship. In addition, Australia does not enfranchise non-citizens at any level of government – apart from British subjects who were on the electoral roll before 1984 – and non-citizens are not eligible for nomination or sitting as a member in local councils, and state, territory and federal parliaments. Most pathways now require at least four years of residency in Australia, and after four years migrants are required to meet several health, education, security and employment requirements in order to be invited to apply for permanent residence.

5 Temporary Migration Experiences: A Case Study

While acknowledging the diversity of migrant experiences from Southeast Asia, migrants were selected for this final section on the basis of achieving a diverse sample of respondents in terms of gender, age, birthplace, ethnicity and religion. For ethical reasons, some aspects of the identities of the participants are not disclosed to protect anonymity. In total, up to 40 temporary migrants from mainland and maritime Southeast Asia, including Cambodia, Vietnam and Indonesia, with varying levels of vulnerability, participated in the study.

In development studies, it is widely understood that social, economic and political progress in development cannot be achieved without the alleviation of vulnerability (Naudé et al., 2009). The concept of vulnerability in development studies has traditionally focused on poverty but has since broadened to include other risk factors such food insecurity, natural hazards and macroeconomic shocks. This study further expands the concept of vulnerability to include political insecurity and exclusion. For this reason, the study recruited migrants identified as having both socio-economic and political vulnerabilities. The latter can be measured not only in terms of not having permanent residency or citizenship but also in terms of not having adequate political representation. Participants from Southeast Asia were included in the study if they were (a) a temporary visa holder, and (b) from a low socio-economic background. The fieldwork also focused on three main origin countries – Cambodia, Indonesia and Vietnam.

As discussed, it is likely that political vulnerabilities may lead to a host of other insecurities which undermine people's ability to realise their capabilities. In the next section, the empirical analysis relies on a mixed method approach that draws on a survey questionnaire with human capability indicators developed by Anand et al. (2009) and semi-structured in-depth interviews. A mixed-methods approach provides insights into the temporary migrant experiences of well-being and vulnerability in Australia. The method of analysis combines quantitative evaluative analysis based on social indicators with a qualitative research design which draws on thematic analysis of the interviews with participants.

The temporary migrants from Southeast Asia were interviewed on a range of capabilities that impact overall health, well-being and long-term security. The migrants selected were drawn from a range of backgrounds in terms of ethnicity, religion, age and gender. As previously discussed, this approach developed by Sen (1985) in *Commodities and Capabilities* and, more recently, by Nussbaum (2011) departs from traditional human economic welfare studies that do not include the things a person could be or do (their 'capabilities'), instead focusing primarily on what temporary migrants actually do. This development studies approach is particularly relevant for temporary migrants who often lack long-term security and the ability to plan a future, which is exacerbated by a lack of bureaucratic responsiveness and accountability.

The survey questionnaire utilises questions that relate to the main themes on Nussbaum's list of human capabilities with a specific focus on political capabilities, subjective well-being and control over one's own environment. The questionnaire was used to start a conversation which was then transcribed and thematically coded. The interviews were conducted in the participants' mother tongue or national language (i.e. Cambodian, Indonesian and Vietnamese) and then later translated into English. This was so that subjective experiences could be fully expressed and communicated in the language that participants are most comfortable with. The respondents placed most weight on the following themes: citizenship and belonging; government responsiveness; participation in politics; political representation; work and skill recognition; equal treatment, dignity and respect; and bodily health and reproductive choice. Excerpts from the survey and in-depth responses are analysed thematically below.

5.1 Citizenship and Belonging

By far the greatest concern for all participants is the uncertainty around the future likelihood of gaining permanent residency or citizenship. Without permanent residency or citizenship temporary migrants find themselves in limbo with no ability to plan for their futures – such as planning for their education, careers, health security and home ownership. This places a great deal of strain on their daily lives. While Australia was once regarded as a settler state which welcomed migrants for permanent settlement, evidently the situation has changed dramatically, with Australia now joining Canada as a country with some of the highest rates of temporary migration as a percentage of annual migration flows among the world's democracies (Boucher & Gest, 2018). We have barely scratched the surface of how this trend is affecting the everyday mental and psychological state of temporary migrants, who live and work in countries like Australia and Canada under a permanent cloud of uncertainty, with absolutely no guarantee of a silver lining.

There are multiple barriers that Southeast Asian migrants face after arrival in Australia, particularly in regard to applying for permanent residency. One recurring concern is that government agencies can restrict access to permanent residency and citizenship by simply not communicating with the visa applicant in a timely manner or, if they do, not provide any reasoning or justification for decisions made. For example, at the time of writing, an Indonesian respondent Novi says that she is still waiting to hear from the federal Department of Home

Affairs after applying over twenty months prior, having spent almost $AU8000 on her temporary visa:

> Until today, I'm still waiting for the answer on my partner visa application but there is nothing I can do other than to wait and look at the updates through my immigration account. The last time I checked, it said '20 months ago'. Again, I understand it is a long process, but it would probably be easier if I knew somebody to ask about the progress of my visa application. I spent around $7,900 for a spouse or partner visa and I have been hoping for news from the Department of Home Affairs regarding my immigration status and I have heard nothing.

Novi's story is not atypical and, like many of the others interviewed for this element, rather complex. After marrying an Australian citizen, Novi left Indonesia and moved to Australia with her husband using a temporary visitor visa. Before getting married, Novi thought that the process for becoming a permanent resident after arrival would be straightforward given that she was married to an Australian citizen. As such, Novi paid around $AU200 to apply for a Visitor visa of three years' duration, with multiple entries. Unfortunately, one of the conditions of her Visitor visa was that she had to leave Australia every three months and then re-enter and was not allowed to work. To avoid this rigmarole, Novi applied for a Partner visa (Temporary, Subclass 820) in November 2019. While waiting for her Partner visa application to go through, she applied for and was granted a Bridging visa A (Subclass 010), which is a temporary visa that generally allows a foreign citizen to stay in Australia after their current substantive visa ceases and while their new substantive visa application is being processed.

Frustrated by the array of visas and applications, all with hefty application fees and lengthy processing delays, Novi has not been reassured by her Indonesian friends who had married Australian citizens and settled in Australia. For many of them, it appears to have been a relatively streamlined process to get permanent residency, while noting that this was five or ten years ago. Searching for more current information, Novi joined a Facebook support group comprising Indonesians in Australia who are waiting for an outcome on their permanent residency applications. Most in the group have been waiting more than two years for an outcome, whether positive or negative. Novi has resigned herself to the fact that she too will most probably be waiting for a full two years in visa and residency limbo, and will need to update multiple supporting documents including health and police checks, all of which cost hundreds of dollars. She will also need to prove that she and her sponsor – her husband – are still married and co-habiting.

Novi's experiences and those among her Facebook support group are one of continuous uncertainty and vulnerability with a level of dependence on their husbands as sponsors. Novi mentioned that among her Facebook friends there were experiences of domestic violence and coercive control at the hands of their sponsoring partner. This is an extremely vulnerable situation for the migrants in question, who are fully dependent on their partners both financially and in terms of residency status, and they are not always aware of who they can turn to for protection, or whether to place their trust in authorities. Moreover, it is difficult to trust authorities when their interaction with government, usually with the stonewall that is the Department of Home Affairs, is a cold and very much dispiriting and one-sided experience. Even worse, the more one tries to assert oneself in communicating with polite yet firm requests to have one's case looked at, to no effect, the more one feels ignored. The cost of the exercise, if perchance it is mentioned in the endless cycles of written communication with government officials in Home Affairs, is not seen as a compelling factor in progressing the application.

In addition to the inordinate costs of extending her temporary visa application while she waits for permanent residency, Truc from Vietnam also refers to the barriers of gaining employment, without sufficient experience in the role or position:

> But there are occupations that require work experience to apply. It used to be more relaxed, I think it was 6 years ago, they wouldn't ask for work experience but because there are a lot of people who are applying, they do that to knock out those who have just graduated. I don't think it is a sustainable policy, I think they just put it in because they want to reduce the number of people and they can make more revenue. Because instead of being able to apply for a 190 visa [Skilled Nominated Visa] directly, now I have to go through a 485 visa [Temporary Graduate Visa], and it costs me another $1600 or $1800.

The impression that the government wants to reduce the number of migrants or deter migrants from submitting permanent residency applications is widespread, with cost a key element of deterrence. Some applicants have additional costs involving migration agents (approximately $AU5000), with others endure the social or opportunity costs of not having a migration agent. For example, Fajar refers to the class divide among temporary migrants between those, on the one hand, who can afford the cost of migration agents or brokers in addition to their visa costs and, on the other, those who cannot afford the extra costs:

> Some people also think that at the end it looks like a business for some people. Those who have money, they will seek the help of an agent to do their visa

application. But that is not cheap. These agents would likely have an inside connection to follow up in the Department of Home Affairs. Just like in Indonesia, sometimes a connection within government departments is needed. The difference is, because Indonesia is our own country, it's easier for us to find a connection that could give us more information. But here, we migrants can't do anything except to wait, because we do not know anyone working in the Australian government.

Here again is a reference to not having access to a personal contact in government, and the frustration that this entails. Dealing with government in Indonesia, Fajar explains, is not nearly as frustrating because one can relatively easily find a contact within the public service who may be in a position, or may know someone in a position, to provide more information or, even better, expedite a positive business transaction. In Australia, it appears, all one can do is wait and hope for the best, regardless of whether a migration agent or broker is involved.

Waiting is stressful in itself. The unresponsive nature of government agencies or officials handling visa or citizenship applications is endemic and, for the applicants, a source of low-level stress. As Fajar observes:

> I must admit that sometimes it is stressful to think about my status here. This is because I've been waiting for more than a year and I haven't heard anything about my visa application. I'm the type of person that makes priorities and life goals, and I try to evaluate them as often as I can.

Anger is also a common emotion, especially with the mounting costs involved. Leaving aside the costs of migration agents, brokers or lawyers, typical costs for temporary migrants in 2021 include the citizenship application fee (approximately $AU500), mandatory medical tests (approximately $AU300) and English language tests (i.e. IELTS) (approximately $AU400), with no guarantee that one can obtain the sufficient academic points needed to support the application. Consider the following observation from Truc, a Vietnamese migrant based in South Australia:

> I felt angry, stupid (retaking IELTS). Number one, IELTS is not enough to accurately reflect one's ability to speak English. Like I can't say, 'look I got a 9 in IELTS and I am an amazing teacher'. I can communicate with my students just fine without an IELTS. And I remember the year before taking IELTS, I was stressed out, because with IELTS they want it in a specific way with writing and reading, it must be in specific way, and it doesn't reflect the way I use English to teach my students. It is another revenue-making exercise because it forces people to take it over and over again, and the government makes more money.

Here, we see the suggestion that the difficulty of the English language tests is linked with revenue raising which, for the migrant applicant, may also be another deterrent. Truc arrived in Australia from Vietnam at the beginning of her secondary high school studies and graduated with a bachelor of education after four years of study. Truc was offered a twelve-month teaching contract in a high school in regional South Australia, followed by a second twelve-month contract in a high school in Adelaide. After a considerable period of education and employment experience, Truc is still required to pass tests that she feels are structured in a way which make it difficult for migrants to pass and apply for permanent residency. Furthermore, the financial costs for the tests, paid up-front, are crippling, with no guarantee of permanent residency or citizenship regardless of the result.

In addition to the English language testing issue, temporary migrants are under considerable pressure to find full-time work experience for up to four years for some visas before they can apply for permanent residency. As Hadi observes, finding full-time employment is very difficult without local networks and connections. For most temporary migrants, the only options for employment are temporary and casual:

> I have struggled to find a full-time job in my time here in Perth because I'm still on a temporary visa, a bridging visa. I think it will need around four years until the permanent visa is granted. Full-time jobs are mostly for permanent residents and citizens, while for those on temporary visas or bridging visas like me, the job opportunities are mostly casual. Full-time jobs are mostly for permanent residents and citizens because companies don't want to take the risk by recruiting a temporary visa holder. You need a good network or connection. Second, you must have work experience in Australia and hold a degree from an Australian institution. In my case, I don't meet the criteria at all.

The ongoing fear that a temporary visa will not be renewed creates considerable anxiety and stress, especially given that most temporary visas do not allow migrants to have access to Australia's universal health insurance scheme (Medicare), which covers medical services by doctors, specialists and other health professionals, hospital treatment, dental care and prescription medicines. A Vietnamese migrant, Lan, describes the incredible strain placed on her family as they await the outcome of their visa applications, which means that, in the interim, they do not have any health, employment or financial security:

> My husband told me that this is the last processing opportunity for us. If we fail, we will not receive any Medicare and we will not be legally allowed to work. We will become illegal workers. So, there are many things to worry about. At the moment we are provided with Medicare with a bridging visa,

but if our application fails this time, Medicare will not be provided for our family. We will be like homeless people. If we do not work, we cannot survive financially. But if we work, we can be arrested at any time. I hope the government can issue our identity papers. We are living in anxiety and worry every day.

Lan also describes the anguish of being on temporary and bridging visas for more than eight years while awaiting an outcome on her family's refugee status. As described above, she is deeply concerned that her family situation will slip into an irregular status while they are waiting for their applications to be processed. This is a terrifying thought for a refugee who has escaped political persecution in her own country:

> Sometimes I am worried that we will be stopped and searched by the police because our papers are still being processed. We are afraid that the police might grab us someday and send us back to Vietnam. We are now staying here without any status so that can happen at any time. We're always waiting on visa extension outcomes.

This reflection highlights a deep fear for many temporary migrants, namely that delays to visa application processing allows the distinct possibility that they may be discovered by the authorities and summarily deported, with little recourse to appeal.

5.2 Government Responsiveness

Government communication channels, ostensibly to promote the processes involved in applying for permanent residency and citizenship, are, according to the migrant participants, cursory and unhelpful, with limited opportunity to actually speak to the relevant officer. A simple phone call from Home Affairs is rare, and government emails are often sent without a signature block containing the officer's full name or contact details. For temporary migrants, this makes them feel politically powerless, as if they are second-class citizens. As observed by Fajar, there is a general impression that the situation, or rather the lack of communication encountered in the application process, is getting worse:

> I've heard also from people's stories that the process is more stringent, compared to a few years ago. But what makes it even harder, I think, is that I don't know who to talk to about following up on my visa application.

The overwhelming sense is that the concerns of temporary migrants are not being taken seriously in the confusing array of policies and regulations that have a disproportionate impact on them, with little to no opportunity to provide comment or feedback, let alone shape the regulatory policies and processes.

There appears to be a distinct lack of institutional accountability, which can be defined as the level of responsiveness of institutions to the interests of those who are subject to their authority (Benton, 2010).

The unresponsiveness of government, whether it be at the state or federal level, is partly related to the fact that governments do not have an immediate electoral incentive to look after the interests of non-citizens, even though they may contribute meaningfully to society as taxpayers, essential workers and community members. For many migrants, elected representatives are perceived as a source of hope. As one participant observes, 'Australian politicians do care about the issues that concern migrants from my background'. Yet while politicians are generally perceived as having the ability to expedite the process, the reality of the situation, and the sense of hopelessness, are stark. In Fajar's words:

> I think that a representative in the parliament that could represent the interests and needs of migrants is important. To be honest, I have no idea of who to talk to regarding my visa status. A link to someone is sometimes needed. If you have a student visa, or tourist visa, you can run to the Consulate General of Indonesia, or Embassy of Indonesia. But with a bridging visa, when you want to ask about your visa application, you can ask for advice, but they can't do much. Neither the Consulate General nor the Embassy have any power in this regard, as the decision in the end is made by the Australian government. I once talked to the Indonesian Consulate General and the Embassy, just to share my experiences, and they gave me a contact to reach out to. But it wasn't a contact of a person to talk to, or a representative that could help me to follow up the progress of my application. I don't know whether it's usual or not to do that but waiting for quite a long period of time for something is very tiring and stressful.

The harsh reality is, everyday policy-making tends to be skewed in favour of citizens (Bellamy, 2007; Benton, 2014), and most politicians will not bend over backwards to assist in visa or immigration matters. This is primarily because of the complexity and politically charged nature of the issue, not to mention that there are few votes, if any, that can be earned from appearing soft on temporary migrants seeking citizenship. Ironically, in cases where temporary migrants are stigmatised by politicians for political advantage, citizenship can safeguard vulnerable stigmatised groups, often denied basic human rights, from being the object of political campaigns. Alas, citizenship is precisely what they lack.

Elected representatives should have longer-term incentives to look after temporary migrants who may one day become citizens or may gain the sympathy and understanding of sections of the voting electorate, for example among those with similar migration, religious or ethnic backgrounds. Temporary migrants have a high level of dependence on government responsiveness and accountability so that they can plan and realise their full capabilities. This is especially the case for migrants where a significant time-period has lapsed and where they are more likely to have developed strong social and emotional ties to their communities (Benton, 2014). Yet for many of the respondents, politicians are regarded with a sense of disappointment or, if not disappointment, disdain. Consider Dian's observations:

> I don't feel that Australian politicians care about us. I think they just care about how much money they are making. It might come across that they care about us, but I think the bottom line is they just think about money. For example, when Covid-19 started in March last year, the university started giving out packages of money. For instance, they might give international students $1000 or $2000 if we showed we were going through a difficult time in terms of finance. But it would have been a better solution to reduce the tuition fees because we couldn't afford the tuition fees without any work or welfare support. I feel they don't really care about us. They come across as not friendly or supportive. I think they just covered themselves to make sure they still get the money in.

The multiple costs of visas are a recurring source of frustration. It also colours many other issues of importance including the willingness, or lack thereof, of politicians to get involved. Chenda, a Cambodian, says that he feels temporary migrants are simply not being taken seriously by the government:

> I think the politicians here do not really care about temporary migrants. I think we are not really welcome politically. It means our political views seem to not be taken seriously. But other views seem to be taken well.

While Southeast Asian migrant views on apolitical issues seem to have a place in Australian society, political views are of no consequence, or are in fact unwelcome. This reflects, to some extent, the way in which temporary migrants overwhelmingly feel accepted by everyday Australian communities, who tend to rally together to welcome new migrants or refugees to help them find their feet, find employment and help their children feel settled in at school. Nevertheless, the very same migrants speak of the way in which the government does not seem to pull its weight, as well as the manner in which they are ignored or unaccepted by Australia's political elites. This may stem from the fact that the goodwill of community or ethnic groups can only go so far. Often there are situations, like finding employment or sorting out urgent visa or health issues, that require the assistance of government.

5.3 Participation in Politics

The need for a voice in politics either through voting or through a representative with a degree of influence and networks in the political system increases for those when the exit costs – that is, costs associated with leaving the country or applying for permanent residency – are prohibitively costly, dangerous or infeasible (Benton, 2014). One way to have a voice formally in politics is through voting in local, state or federal elections. While international law has included previously disenfranchised groups such as women and Indigenous groups, it has not had any say on non-citizens, leaving the decisions of who can be included in the *demos* to democratic states (Arrighi & Bauböck, 2017).

Democratic theorists have argued that those subject to the laws that affect them should have voting rights, relying on a principle of residence rather than nationality. That is, nationality is based on place of birth, referred to as *Ius Soli* or one's descendants, referred to as *Ius Sanguinis* (López-Guerra, 2005; Owen, 2012; Bauböck, 2015). Overall, there is emerging evidence of a post-national conception of the *demos* with voting rights for non-citizens usually restricted to nationals now being expanded to include long-term non-citizens. However, the expansion of the *demos* tends to be limited to local and state elections (Arrighi & Bauböck, 2017). In some developing countries, non-citizens are encouraged to vote because their size, background and political preferences are likely to influence political outcomes. For example, undocumented migrants from Indonesia and the Philippines have long been encouraged to vote in elections in the Malaysian state of Sabah in northern Borneo (Sadiq, 2005; Frank, 2006).

In Australia, state governments are responsible for health, education, industrial relations, community services, policing and emergency services, involving laws and policies that directly impact the lives of temporary migrants in terms of their experiences with health, education, employment conditions and justice outcomes. However, most laws and policies relating to immigration and citizenship fall under the responsibility of the federal government. The concerns of temporary migrants, therefore, cut across state and federal government responsibilities. When Southeast Asian temporary migrants were asked whether they should be allowed to vote in elections, there was a mixed response, depending on factors such as political knowledge and length of stay in Australia. Several respondents felt that it would make a difference to be able to vote in the local, state and federal elections. For example, Seyha from Cambodia said that she would like policies to consider her interests as a temporary migrant:

> In terms of elections, I want to have the right to vote in local, state and federal elections. It is because everything policy-wise will affect me personally in

this country. I need representatives to make policies that take my concerns seriously.

Again, we see evidence of a need to be afforded the right to a political voice, not least because this would allow some say in shaping the policies that affect migrants. Some migrants feel that the length of time living in Australia should be taken into consideration in whether a migrant should be granted political rights. For example, one of the Indonesian respondents, Iwan, said that permanent residents should be able to vote because they have usually lived in the country for a long time, and voting will help to encourage interest and participation in politics. In Iwan's words:

> I would be happy to participate if one day the Australian government allows permanent residents to vote in the country because permanent residents will stay in Australia for quite a long time. I don't think they'll stay just for a short period of time. In that regard, it's good to involve permanent residents to vote. They should understand the politics in Australia. We might assume that a permanent resident doesn't know much about Australian politics and seems to not care about it but that's because we are not involved. If permanent residents are given the right to vote, they'll take responsibility to take part in politics, including understanding the politics in Australia. I don't think they'll stay quiet, particularly when there's a policy that may be threatening their security. The right to politics will give people more responsibility to be involved in politics.

The majority of respondents agreed that they should have rights to vote in local and state elections, as opposed to federal elections, as they feel they have more understanding of the local policies and laws that are more likely to have a personal impact on them. Others, meanwhile, felt that migrants should have the right to vote because their presence has a role to play in Australian society and, in the context of the pandemic, Australia's Covid-19 response. Consider the comments below from Phi, a Vietnamese migrant:

> When I am a migrant and I live here, it means I am part of Australia. I am working and studying here and everything I do here will have some impact on Australia. For example, when migrants are living here, they are using the services, paying the bills, paying rent and fees. They should have rights. For example, during a difficult time such as during the Covid pandemic time, they should be equal to Australians.

As we can see, there are many reasons why temporary migrants feel that they should be allowed the right to vote. However, by the same token, there is not a great deal of agreement at which level of government, which type of migrant and for what reasons voting should be allowed.

As previously discussed, many temporary migrants live in precarious situations with very little political agency and control over their own environment. Nussbaum (2011) shows the importance of being able to participate effectively in political choices that govern one's life. Nearly all respondents acknowledged that decisions made at local and state levels have an influence on the lives of temporary migrants. Many also felt that it was their sense of responsibility to be informed and involved in the political decisions that impact them and their communities. Consider the following comments from Fajar:

> In my opinion, it's important to understand policies made by the government that affect you. Not only as migrants, but also as someone who lives in Australia, even if only for a short period of time. Decisions made at the local and state level influence us a lot, whether we are citizens or not. As long as we live in the area, we have to obey the rules no matter what our status is in Australia. So, I think, non-citizens should be allowed to show their preferences through voting.

Underlining previous observations on voting in local or state government elections, some such as Retno see these second- and third-tier levels of government as having the greatest impact on the rights of migrants:

> If one day non-citizens here are eligible to vote, I think it's alright only for the local and state elections because these closely affect us. So, I think the local and state governments have a big impact and migrants could vote to choose their preferences based on who they think will bring them better conditions.

Others, such as Yudi, an Indonesian migrant worker, are of the opinion that because voting is not allowed for any temporary migrants, as a concession, voting could be allowed in local and state elections, as this is better than nothing:

> I do wish that I could participate in elections, especially local and state elections. Although we are not citizens, we have lived here for a long time. Some of us might also consider applying for citizenship. Those of us who have lived here for a long time already feel like we are Australian.

There are nuances to this argument, however. Consider the following observation from Sari, who feels that while voting at the local or state level should be encouraged, non-citizens should *not* be granted the right to vote in national elections:

> I think migrants who are not citizens, but who may be a permanent resident or willing to be a citizen, can be given the right to vote in the local and state elections. The decisions made at these two levels will affect their livelihood while they live here. No matter what your status is here, decisions made by the

mayor and premier will influence migrants. For example, when [Queensland Premier] Annastacia Palaszczuk made a decision regarding Covid, that applied to everyone, not just citizens. In that regard, I think it is important for non-citizens to understand the politics in their own region, to know who's the candidate, and to participate in the election. Non-citizens who plan to stay longer here should be given the rights to politics in their region. However, I don't think non-citizens should be given the right to vote in the federal election. I think it's a bigger context. There are things at the federal level that might not be of relevance to non-citizens, or non-citizens are just not interested. Besides, they're still attached to their home country, which may lead to bias. In the federal election, I think voting rights should only be given to citizens.

This reluctance to support voting rights at the national level appears to stem from a concern that temporary migrants will somehow not be fully loyal to Australia. As Yudi explains, there is an acknowledgement that they are conflicted at the national level, as there is a belief that the national government tends to work in the international or multilateral sphere:

I think it would be nice to be given political rights, especially at the local and state level. I'm not sure with the federal elections though, because our status is not as a citizen, and decisions made at the federal level can also be about relations between states.

In contrast to the observations revealed above, some respondents were reluctant to vote in Australian elections at any level. This is primarily because they felt that they had not lived in Australia long enough or had little interest in Australian politics. Consider the following from Pheakdey, a Cambodian temporary migrant:

I think I should not vote in the local election. I don't have much knowledge about the politicians and the political system. What I want may not reflect the reality because I don't have much knowledge about it. But if I live here longer, like say 5 years or more, I think I should vote. This is because I would have more knowledge about the country and the public service.

Nevertheless, as outlined above, the overwhelming response from respondents is that they wanted to have the same political rights as citizens when it comes to voting in local and state elections. Some respondents even went a step further by arguing that long-term migrants should have the right to vote in elections at all levels of government. Consider the following observations from Wulan, an Indonesian respondent:

I don't think migrants on a temporary visa should be involved in voting. Those with permanent visas could vote in local and state elections, but not in the federal elections. I think people in the federal level of government think more of high political issues such as wars, foreign policy, and others. These policies may affect non-citizens, but they do not directly influence their daily life, and they will not stay here forever. Because I think you need to be a smart voter nowadays. You have to have a good reason for your preferences; why you like the candidate, why do you want to vote for them, what do you expect from them. The decisions made at the federal level do not directly influence you. Decisions made by the mayor or by the premier, those are the policies and regulations that will influence you. So, migrants should probably vote in the local and state elections, but not in federal elections.

This reluctance to consider migrant voting at the national level appears to stem from the notion that the national government is more concerned with international relations, as opposed to local or domestic issues.

5.4 Political Representation

Even though there were mixed feelings among respondents when it comes to voting, nearly all were enthusiastic about having a well-informed political representative who they could talk to. They were of the belief that this would make a significant difference in being able to fulfil their capabilities. In particular, many conveyed the hope that migrants with similar backgrounds may make a difference to their everyday circumstances, if they were to become an elected representative. Consider the following comments, from Retno:

> I think it's a good thing. Especially if, maybe, we could have an Indonesian who moved to Australia and became a citizen, in the parliament. I don't think I have heard of one like that. But if that's not possible, at least someone with a good background understanding of migrants or Indonesia. It's good to have a representative who understands our position, especially people like me who are still waiting for an improved visa or citizenship status from the department of immigration.

Of course, not all temporary migrants feel that a political representative with a migrant background needs to share their particular nationality. As Sari observes:

> If we are talking about political representatives, I agree that there should be some with a migrant background. But anyone can represent us Indonesian migrants – they don't need to be an Indonesian, it can even be an Anglo, the main thing is they have the ability to represent the interests of migrants.

Wulan expressed the hope that an Indonesian with Australian citizenship in parliament would understand and advocate not only for the unique Indonesian migrant experience but also for minorities in general, including Muslims:

> I agree that migrants should have representation in the parliament, someone who could represent the interest of migrants. I'm imagining someone like an

Australian citizen with an Indonesian background. It would be nice to have an
Indonesian representative in the parliament, to advocate for the needs of us
minorities here, including Indonesians and Muslims. There are many issues that
us migrants face, but sometimes because we're non-White, we feel like our
voices are not heard. I know many Indonesian friends here who still struggle to
get citizenship, even to get a permanent visa. They could raise their concerns
with a representative, and that may help them, to ease the way. It's good to know
that in Australia we are free to raise our voices, in any way. But I doubt that our
voices are heard, I'm not sure that they are. Because I personally think that as
long as we are non-White, we are in the minority. With a representative who has
similar experiences, it would be much better, and we would feel more at home.

Luki, who is aware of several migrants from China and India elected to
parliament, expressed a similar sentiment:

I think it would be nice to one day have an Indonesian Muslim who is an
Australian citizen to sit in the parliament. Living for a long time here, I have
never heard of one who is in the parliament, or even at the local or state level.
I've seen Chinese, Indians, I think. There are quite a large number of Muslim
Indonesians in Australia, and many more people might come and become
permanent residents here.

Respondents from mainland Southeast Asia share similar hopes, albeit without the call for an elected official to represent Muslim interests. Pheakdey
eloquently conveyed his hopes in the following way:

It would be good to have a representative from our own country. He or she
can represent us and bring our concerns to be discussed in parliament. It
would be good to have someone to talk to. I think it would be great to have
a Cambodian representative in the Australian parliament. I really want this
to happen. I think the politicians here don't really care about us. The
government does not seem to care. The government puts their own citizens
first.

A Vietnamese respondent conveyed the same ideas using a pertinent analogy:

I think it is like in school or university, we always have a class representative
for international students, and if you generalise that, I think we should have
a representative for temporary migrants or migrants in general. I would say
probably someone who is a migrant themselves or used to be migrant, maybe
someone who has studied Australian politics, went to a university, worked in
the political field themselves and stayed connected with migrants.

These opinions are significant, highlighting the capacity of migrants not only to
settle and contribute to Australian society but also to play a key role in engender-
ing political trust among migrant or Muslim communities. Comparative research
has shown that political representation is known to increase levels of trust,

confidence and feelings of political efficacy among those who have been trad-itionally under-represented (Morales, 2009; Pietsch, 2018). Representation is especially important when pan-ethnic groups of migrants feel that their concerns about laws and policies which directly have an impact on their daily lives have been unheard and unrepresented in the political system. As mentioned previously, there is a perception that governments are largely unresponsive, incommunicative and unaccountable when it comes to temporary migrant concerns about their visa status and applications for permanent residency.

The respondents in this study consistently demonstrate that temporary migrants are especially vulnerable and dependent on government when it comes to their legal status within the country. This dependency on government is a particular concern for migrants as, due to their lack of citizenship or personal political connections, they do not feel a connection with local members of parliament as representatives of the major political parties. Yet they are acutely aware of how much they need parliamentarians. Lia, one of the Indonesian respondents, describes the situation in the following way:

> Although I don't agree that new migrants should be required to vote, I agree that migrants should have representatives in parliament. A few days ago, my husband shared some information with me about budget cutting in Centrelink. If I'm not mistaken, it says that family benefits, childcare, maternity leave, and other kinds of subsidies from the government will be cut for non-permanent residents. If that happens, it would be hard for us. We need around four years to get our permanent visa. Does that mean that we need to wait for four years to have a baby? As new migrants, our life has been hard already. For example, job markets are limited for us. If we have representatives in the parliament, maybe we would know who to talk to. Now, we don't know who we can rely on or talk to if we have concerns. I don't know if currently there's any Australian politicians who have a heart for temporary migrants, I've never heard of any.

Some migrants acknowledge that while a local member is needed to stand up for their rights, they might not be able to be approached due to the language barrier. Hong, a Vietnamese migrant, says that:

> I consider myself to be lucky, having an education at the university level and having a good command of English. But for the parents of my friends who came here on guardian visas, they are old and do not know English and do not know how to deal with a situation when it arises. They might not be aware that they are doing something illegal according to Australian law. In such cases, we need representatives to protect our rights.

Even with perfect English, understanding that an elected representative can advocate for migrant rights is only one part of a complex equation. Not having a personal connection with a local politician or elected official is yet another barrier to inclusion. Culturally, knowing who to talk to in politics or government is incredibly important for migrants. This can be more relevant for temporary migrants than the average Australian citizen, because their lives are so heavily dependent on the goodwill of local ethnic or community groups and, in particular, having personal connections with the key contacts in those groups who can provide the best assistance. The heightened importance of personal connections in the political sphere, or lack thereof, is an extension of this more practical and personable way of getting things done.

As the comments above indicate, Southeast Asian migrants hold high hopes for democratically elected officials who they believe can advocate for migrants, based on their own migrant experience. Statistically, the widespread existence of officials with such an experience should be a reality. First- and second-generation migrants now account for 44 per cent of the population, making Australia one of the most diverse immigrant democracies in the world (Kwok & Pietsch, 2017a; Pietsch, 2017a, 2018). A comparatively large proportion of Australia's population, approximately 17 per cent, is from a non-white migrant or ethnic minority background. The largest group in this category are first- and second-generation migrants from Asia, referred to here as 'Asian-Australians', which make up more than 14 per cent of Australian population. Asian-Australians are also the fastest-growing group among the pan-racial minority categories. Therefore, it makes a great deal of practical sense, both politically and strategically, to have elected representatives who, based on their lived experience of migration, embody a more diverse range of views.

Similar arguments have been made for the inclusion of women and minority groups in government and political institutions. According to Kim (2005, p. 451), 'a diverse workforce with regards to race, ethnicity, national origin, or gender leads a bureaucracy to be not only internally democratic but also responsive to citizen needs'. Reflecting this, those with a relatively recent experience of migration or racism are more likely to make a stand on changes to legislation and policies that have a disproportionate impact on migrants and ethnic communities (Pietsch, 2018, 2020). Some respondents indicated that certain politicians do precisely this, whether or not they have a migrant background. In Fajar's words:

> I have seen that Australian politicians do care about migrants. At the start of the Covid pandemic there was a politician, I have forgotten her name, but I saw it in the news, she publicly advocated for foreigners with student visas who happened to be stuck in Australia to be granted the right to continue working in Australia in order to continue with their lives here. In effect, this advocacy meant that workers and students with temporary visas who were

stuck in the wrong state after border closures, were allowed to cross the border and work in another state, where there was work. In my case, I was granted permission to work in Victoria when I was stuck there.

As mentioned previously, very few Australian politicians will look out for temporary migrants. This is mainly because, politically, it is a risk. This is why it is so important to have migrants involved in politics at the highest levels of policy decision-making. After all, migrants have a unique insight into the lived experience of migration including the navigation of migration pathways and settlement, and responding to systemic exclusion and unconscious bias. As one respondent says, 'we are outsiders and we can have fresh and unbiased viewpoints which can contribute to local policies and can make a better balance in a world where there is lots of racism and discrimination'.

I have argued elsewhere that the recruitment of more ethnic minority candidates can enhance a political party's appeal to ethnic diverse electorates and the overall legitimacy of the political system (Pietsch, 2017a, 2017b). However, there are significant barriers to the recruitment of Asian or other candidates from minority backgrounds. One key stumbling block is the factional processes involved in political party candidate recruitment and selection mechanisms. These processes are secretive, given MPs are reluctant to discuss the mechanisms underpinning candidate selection processes, especially when there are warring factions to consider (Pietsch, 2017a). This issue surfaced in September 2021 when Australian Labor Party (ALP) senator Kristina Keneally announced her plan to move to the lower house by running in a safe, multicultural seat, displacing a local candidate with a Vietnamese refugee background, Tu Le. The plan was for Kristina Keneally, who resides on an exclusive island offshore from Sydney's affluent Northern Beaches, to move to the seat of Fowler in Sydney's west, replacing retiring MP Chris Hayes. Hayes, however, had publicly supported local lawyer Tu Le to replace him in representing the multicultural electorate, which Labor holds with a strong 14 per cent margin. Labor MP Anne Aly – the first Muslim woman elected to the Australian parliament – says the move to parachute Kristina Keneally into the seat is a 'huge failure for Labor on diversity' (Karp & Remeikis, 2021). Aly called out her party's hypocrisy:

> Diversity, equality and multiculturalism can't just be a trope that Labor pulls out and parades while wearing a sari and eating some Kung Pao chicken to make ourselves look good. For the Labor party to be in a position where they are pushing aside a community representative from one of the most multicultural electorates is hypocrisy as far as I'm concerned (AAP, 2021).

In a similar vein, Osmond Chiu, who has led a grassroots push to improve diversity in NSW Labor, said that 'much of this underlying angst and anger isn't about Senator Keneally herself and whether she'd be a good local MP. It's about what it symbolises: if diversity doesn't matter for the most multi-cultural seat in Australia, it suggests it never did to begin with' (Karp & Remeikis, 2021).

Understandably, Tu Le has expressed disappointment at not being considered for the seat. Even more dismaying, Le ticks all the boxes. She is a woman, of Vietnamese background – her parents having arrived in Australia as refugees – and has been involved in grassroots political activism for years under the tutelage of Chris Hayes, one of the ALP's most respected and hardworking local members. One cannot imagine a more suitable candidate for the seat, given nearly 20 per cent of the electorate are of Vietnamese origin and over 25 per cent were born in Asia (Pietsch, 2017a). The issue has split the ALP, with critics echoing Anne Aly by arguing that Labor is sacrificing diversity for the sake of political expediency (see, for example, Haydar, 2021; Karp & Remeikis, 2021; Worthington, 2021).

It is important to note that a candidate such as Tu Le is exceptional in many ways. Elsewhere, I have argued that Asian migrants from a variety of ethnic backgrounds simply do not see themselves in parliament in the same way that European migrants do (Pietsch, 2017a). Instead, given Asian migrants tend to live in safe Labor seats such as Fowler, they have traditionally relied on their representatives within the ALP such as Chris Hayes or Ed Husic to address their concerns. There are exceptions of course, such as Labor's Senate leader Penny Wong. Speaking of his party's 'diversity credentials' at the height of the Kristina Keneally furore, Labor leader Anthony Albanese stated that 'We have, in western Sydney, people like Ed Husic, the first Muslim elected to the House of Representatives. And we have Anne Aly in the [West Australian] seat of Cowan. We have enormous diversity in our ranks – and guess what? At the next election there's someone called "Albanese" running for prime minister. And in terms of diversity, that's a first too' (Worthington, 2021).

Some commentators were unimpressed by the Labor leader's political spin, given Kristina Keneally herself was born in the United States to an Australian-born mother and, in that sense, can also be classed as a migrant success story. According to the former Race Discrimination Commissioner Tim Soutphommasane, Australia is well behind the United States, Canada, and New Zealand when it comes to multicultural representation: 'It's a dismal state of affairs. Not to put too fine a point on it, but our parliament looks like it belongs in the White Australia era. It's hardly the stuff of "the most successful multicultural society in the world"' (Remeikis, 2021).

On the one hand, having a handful of diversity voices in federal parliament such as Penny Wong, Ed Husic and Anne Aly is an important step forward in making symbolic change. On the other hand, in order to make substantive policy changes that address racism as well as promote the benefits of diversity and migrant inclusion as a source of social and economic strength, a stronger collective voice is needed. While an elected parliamentarian with an affinity for migrants based on personal experience such as Tu Le would be an incredibly valuable political asset, for a truly representative and reinvigorated political culture, more substantive change at a groundswell level, from the bottom up, is needed. This is because the notion of dealing only with a migrant politician is, more or less, an expression of 'personality politics', that is, a politics focused on the personality, rather than political parties or party-aligned policies. This is another critical point in the nexus between migration and political representation, as elected parliamentarians more often than not operate within the constraints of their party's political values. For this reason, local elected members need to be doing much more than shaking hands in their electorate. In addition, they need to be seasoned politicians with some measure of influence in the party room, and comfortable with endlessly cultivating strong links with the party leader, senior party members, up-and-coming party members and the relevant political staffers.

Even if a local member has a measure of gravitas or influence within the party room, they are also to some extent hamstrung by the limitations of the party itself. While political parties are the central institutions of representative democracy, their democratic linkage function is only reserved for linking citizens to government and government policies (Dalton et al., 2011). Parties themselves cannot advocate for a particular migrant who may have missed their visa application or renewal deadline. It is only when citizens collectively advocate and vote on behalf of non-citizens that parties give substantive attention to the concerns of temporary migrants. This means that temporary migrants are highly dependent on the goodwill and understanding of local sympathetic communities and advocacy groups, who are often similarly marginalised within the political mainstream.

5.5 Work and Skill Recognition

A persistent theme in the interviews was that without permanent residency or citizenship, respondents lacked a sense of control over their environment, whether it was the ability to purchase a house, find employment, study or start family planning. Having a sense of control over one's environment is an important capability in Nussbaum's list of bare minimum central capabilities (Nussbaum, 2011). Without permanent residency or citizenship, opportunities for secure employment – not to mention employment that adequately recognises one's skills and talents – are often blocked by the temporary status of their visa or the lack of government communication on the progress of their permanent visa applications. Wolff and De-Shalit (2007) emphasise the importance of 'capability security', where governments not only provide people with a capability but also provide it in a way that allows them to have the ability to plan for their future. Wolff and De-Shalit (2007) argue that this is particularly important for new migrants where security and an ability to plan for the future are of overwhelming importance and is related to other capabilities such as 'emotional health' and 'self-respect', which are important in terms of social and political inclusion.

Wolff and De-Shalit (2007) also argue that 'emotional health' and 'self-respect' can be dependent on removing non-material forms of disadvantage such as dominance, servility and shame. Unfortunately, the relationship between government and temporary migrants is frequently characterised by narratives of dominance and servility, as well as a sense of shame when life and career ambitions are unable to be achieved. In addition to the lack of security and decision-making capability to plan for the future, some temporary visas require applicants to be living in regional areas where there are skills shortages in farming or meat and meat product processing. While this may be of great benefit to the businesses in question, temporary migrants report feeling even more isolated than usual in regional and rural areas, with an increased likelihood of facing discrimination and career barriers (Guan & Pietsch, 2022). In the words of Truc, he feels his life is 'quite uncertain':

> I don't know where I am going to work next year or what state I am going to.
> On a temporary visa, it is hard for me to get permanent job.

Besides the uncertainty due to the lack of capability security, temporary migrants also face the inability to secure permanent or even part-time employment in their chosen field due to their visa regulations, as well as inadequate skills and qualifications recognition. They also face the usual hurdles to employment, including lack of experience. For example, a Cambodian graduate Sokphal says that:

> I constantly feel worried about my PR application. My purpose to come here was to apply for PR and live here. Now I have graduated from the University of Queensland. My major is in engineering management. Now I am looking for an employer who can sponsor me. My visa will expire next year but employers do not want to sponsor me. One more thing is that I study engineering management, but I am working as a chef. It is a big disappointment if I don't get PR. My big challenge is that I don't have experience here in Australia, even if I have experience back home. We need a license or qualification to work here, but my qualification in Cambodia is not legitimate

and is invalid in Australia. My chance to get a license here is slim, so my chance to get a job here is also slim. To be an engineer, I need a license. When I applied to be a salesman in a company that sells engineering products, they need practical experience here. I don't have experience here.

The following account, from Lia, an Indonesian based in Perth, Western Australia (WA), tells a similar story. The impact of lack of experience, inadequate qualifications and visa uncertainty are recurring themes:

> Based on my experience as a new migrant in Australia – literally new as I just moved here last year – there are at least two points that I think are important to get a full-time job. First, you need a good network or connection and second you must have employment experience in Australia and hold a degree from an Australian institution. In my case, I don't meet those criteria, at all. Full-time jobs are mostly for permanent residents and citizens because companies don't want to take the risk of recruiting temporary visa holders. What if one day I leave Australia, what if suddenly you get deported? They just don't want to take that kind of risk and prefer to recruit permanent visa holders, or even citizens. That's what I see in Perth. Recruitment is skill-based, but you need someone that opens doors for you to enter the full-time job market.

Not unlike the hope placed in elected members of parliament described above, Lia is optimistic that a well-placed connection may help her get her foot in the door. Relying on friends and family, or the goodwill of already stretched community groups, of course, is a well-trodden route for migrants and refugees.

Migrants often have little other option other than rely on their own communities, considering the multiple hurdles they face at every turn. For instance, as described in the following account by Chanthou, a Cambodian on a temporary student visa with a young family and looking for work in the State of Queensland, even the simple matter of obtaining a driver's license can be an almost-insurmountable barrier:

> There is one time I applied to upgrade my driving license to a Queensland driving license. I have a driving license from my own country. I applied to take the driving test and failed. Then I am not allowed to drive, even though I still have my driving license from my own country. Now I am not allowed to drive anymore. When I applied, there was no public information about such practices. The officials did not inform me about the consequences of failing the test. I think it is the responsibility of the officials to inform me about the consequences. I want to get the Queensland driving license because it provides me with more security for my family and some jobs require that we have a Queensland driving license.

The entire experience entrenched this migrant's lack of security capability, given that his young family depend on his driver's license, not only for mobility but also for future employment prospects. Even worse, he perceived that he was being discriminated against, in a way that Australian citizens might not be, creating a sense of 'us and them':

> I don't understand why I am not allowed to drive a car and my Cambodian national driving license was invalid after I failed the test. I could drive normally before I took the test and it was deemed legal. It is illogical to invalidate my license. I paid for that service. Some rules are discriminatory. I am not sure about the rules applied to the citizen. But whatever it is, I do think that it is better than what happened to me. I want the same treatment. I don't want to be treated differently. When I applied to take the test, I had a different process, like the requirement to do it over the phone. But for citizens, they can just apply online, which is more convenient. It is not easy to book the driving test by phone. I had to wait on hold for a long time, feeling frustrated. It is inconvenient. It's like I am a second-class citizen.

A common complaint among the respondents was that the employment options open to them in Australia are incompatible with what was promised to them before they decided to work or study in Australia. This, too, feels like a form of discrimination. Consider the following account from Sokha, a Cambodian migrant:

> When I look for a job, there is often a requirement that only candidates with citizenship can apply. This cuts me out as a fresh graduate from overseas. Even though the job is unrelated to national security interests in Australia, there is such a policy. This policy is discriminatory. I want to gain experience in a particular sector, but it's impossible. It's against the objectives of most international students who want to have the best education and gain experience working in Australia. But most jobs require citizenship. If we want to apply for permanent residence and don't have experience, it's impossible for us. When I applied for a visa to study in Australia, I stated clearly in my personal statement that I want to gain practical experience in Australia. It is very different to what I expected.

During the Covid-19 pandemic, Australia's strict border control measures denied entry to non-citizens, including international students enrolled at Australian universities. As a consequence, many international students – through no fault of their own – have been unable to finish their half-completed degrees or engage in post-degree employment or internships, at great personal expense and through no fault of their own.

As pressure grows to find employment before their visa runs out, temporary migrants often have little option other than to leave the city to look for employment. In fact, this is encouraged. In settler countries such as Australia, with a focus on skilled migration, governments have often provided a number of incentives to encourage new migrants to move from urban areas of high immigrant and ethnic concentration to regional and rural areas where there are skills and labour shortages and stagnated population growth (Hugo, 2008). In Australia there has been an increase in regionally sponsored skilled migrants as a proportion of the permanent migration program, increasing from 2 per cent in 1997–1998 to 32 per cent in 2018–2019 (Hugo, 2008; Department of Home Affairs, 2019). Since the Covid-19 pandemic, with negligible permanent migration, this percentage has risen significantly.

Large immigrant-receiving countries such as Australia have increasingly focused on skilled migration not only because of labour shortages but also because of the perception that the public are more in favour of skilled versus unskilled labour (Boucher, 2020) and that migrants with high human capital can easily integrate (Castles, 1992; Hartwich, 2011). Furthermore, many of Australia's regional areas are experiencing population decline (RAI, 2018). The Regional Australia Institute (RAI) argues that 'the scaling up of locally-led migration strategies that are flexible, fit for place, and better equipped to meet local labour needs should be a priority in future immigration, settlement and regional development policies' (RAI, 2018). In recent years, various state nomination and regional sponsored temporary migration visas have been introduced where migrants are obligated to stay in regional areas for at least two years (Department of Home Affairs, 2021). This includes, for instance, employer and state-sponsored regional skilled migration visas (i.e. Skilled Work Regional (Provisional) Subclass 491 visa).

While such policies may reap economic benefits, there has been little research focus on the social impact of these broad economic and political shifts. For example, it is often in the cities – that is, areas of residential concentration and ethnic clustering – where migrants have greater access to a wide variety of supports that assist with their integration and, for many, transition to permanent residency citizenship. Among the many benefits include living close to government services, the ability to develop family and neighbourhood networks and to maintain their own languages and cultures (Haas et al., 2019). In doing so, they contribute to the cultural-syncretism and enrichment of urban cities and improve their chances of upward socio-economic mobility. In contrast, for regional and rural areas in Australia that were previously less exposed to immigration, there is a long tradition of suspicion towards new migrants and racism lingering from the White Australia period (Jupp & Pietsch, 2018).

Geographically, the population in Australia's capital cities and regional areas are patterned with very different features. Cities and regional areas are disproportionately populated, with unequal exposure to migrants and different levels of cultural diversity. The Australian population is highly concentrated in cities with over two-thirds of residents living in a capital city. Migrants are more concentrated in cities than the general Australian population (ABS, 2017b). In 2016, 83 per cent of the overseas-born population lived in a capital city compared with 61 per cent of people born in Australia (ABS, 2017b). Sydney had the largest overseas-born population in Australia, closely followed by Melbourne. In the years after the White Australia Policy was dismantled, between 1975 and 2000, the regional and remote rural areas of Australia could still be classified as fairly 'White' or 'Anglo'. These areas have only had limited experiences accommodating migrants, with a long tradition of endemic racism and anti-immigrant sentiments (Jupp, 2018).

Not surprisingly, it is a big step for a temporary migrant to move from the relative comfort and security of the city to the uncertainty of regional and rural areas. Many issues need to be considered before taking the plunge. As Chenda, a Cambodian migrant based in Brisbane, observes:

> My future goal is to get PR. I feel stressed. I don't know what to do to get PR. I came here to study and get PR. Now I am living in Brisbane. If I want to have a better chance, I can move to the regional area. But it is hard to live in the regional area. It's hard to find a job. This makes everything very complicated and uncertain. I am not sure if I can get PR in the regional area without a job. The government wants us to live in the regional area. The government wants us to spend money there and develop there. It brings benefits to that area. But my PR application is based on a score system, and even if I move to the regional area, my PR success is still uncertain. The government needs to have a guarantee for us to get PR if we move to the regional area. Thus, my future is unclear. The current government's policy is unfair. It worries me. I keep thinking about it every day.

As this account conveys, even if migrants leave the city to find a job, this may have no correlation with their journey to permanent residency or citizenship. In fact, moving to the country may significantly delay their citizenship application. It is a calculated risk. On the one hand, moving to work as a fruit picker or abattoir worker can be of great financial assistance to migrants and their families. The regional economy also experiences significant economic benefits. The remittances can also benefit the country of origin, a key part of the migrant worker so-called double or triple win. On the other hand, temporary migrants inadvertently remove themselves from their family and broader community support networks, not to mention access to government. There is also evidence to suggest that migrants, particularly those from non-European backgrounds, face various forms of racial and ethnic prejudice in their daily lives in rural and regional Australia

(Guan & Pietsch, 2022). Consider the following account from Hadi, a Muslim Indonesian who spent some time working in rural Australia:

> As a migrant, I admit that sometimes I got stressed, because sometimes I got a boss that is racist and it made me depressed. Some people in the regions have never seen non- Australians, never seen a stranger. This affects their point of view towards migrants, towards non-English speakers. They tend to hate non-Australians because they rarely move out of the regions.

As Hadi explains, even those who have been living and working in rural areas for a long period of time experience everyday racism:

> There's a probability that I might experience violence or discrimination in the future, especially considering that I live in a rural town. In my opinion, people in rural areas are not as friendly as Australians in the big cities, who see migrants often. People out here, seem to have xenophobia, and I feel like they don't accept us. They accept us only because they need us. 'Professional worker', is their attitude.

Hadi's observations on racial prejudice in rural and regional Australia, also known colloquially as 'the outback', aligns with more recent studies that have suggested that migrants are less likely to be exposed to racial prejudice and discrimination in neighbourhoods of high ethnic concentration (Pettigrew & Tropp, 2006, 2011), which overwhelmingly tend to be in cities. While racist behaviours – and their causal factors – will be discussed in more depth shortly, suffice to say at this point that the short-term financial benefits of working in rural localities may have long-term negative consequences, in terms of both being a target of anti-immigrant sentiment and the loss of career opportunities (Guan & Pietsch, 2022).

It is worth noting that in relation to temporary Southeast Asian migrants in Australia, there are always outliers and not every move to the country is imbued with negative experiences. For instance, Ngoc, a Vietnamese respondent, left the security of the mainland and its cities to seek employment in regional Tasmania. Her decision appears to have paid off in terms of finding employment, even though she is not using her qualifications and experience:

> It is a fun fact that I am now a full-time chef who cooks Australian cuisine working in Tasmania. This is a little bit different, but you know it is very hard in Australia to find an occupation related to the set of experience that you've already got. It must be four or five years that I have been working as a chef.

It appears that Ngoc has undertaken a variation on what many migrants have done throughout Australia's history, namely heading out beyond the cities and establishing a Chinese, Vietnamese or Malaysian restaurant, and embedding themselves in a small country town, for better or worse. Many have been successful in their business enterprise, working in their own modest way to change or soften anti-immigrant attitudes, which appear to be deeply ingrained. To this day, almost every Australian country town, no matter how small or unassuming, has a well-established Chinese or Asian-fusion restaurant or two. This may have played a modest role in diluting racial prejudice. For instance, in studies of Hispanic migration to the USA, researchers have found that anti-immigrant sentiment is muted when the native-born Anglo population become accustomed to interacting with ethnically diverse populations that speak different languages and have different customs (Lichter et al., 2012).

5.6 Racism, Equal Treatment and Respect

The experience of discrimination and being treated differently can impact people's sense of human dignity and the ability to flourish in the future (Nussbaum, 2019). Human dignity is a central theme in political conceptions of social and global justice. A lack of human dignity can undermine one's overall health and happiness. The respondents provide many accounts of unprovoked racism and incivility directed at Southeast Asian temporary migrants. They feel they are being looked at differently on public transport and in the streets of major capital cities. In Lia's words:

> I feel safe living in Perth. But once, when I went out with two of my friends in the city, someone shouted at us 'go back to your country!' We were surprised. Since then, I always think that in the future I might experience similar things. At first, I thought Australia was a safe country to live in. I never imagined that I would experience that.

Almost all respondents reported racist hostility in everyday situations. Research has shown that Australia has struggled to move on from its White Australia past, suggesting that racial prejudice, especially towards non-white racial minorities, could still be a determinant of anti-immigrant sentiment in regional areas of low population density (Jupp, 2018; Pietsch, 2018). Consider the following account, which is by no means unusual, from a Cambodian, Chanthou:

> There are some racism issues I have personally encountered. One day I drove my car from my house to the corner of the street. Suddenly, one man driving in a car almost hit my car and shouted out to me 'F–k you'. He saw me in the car with my kids and he saw me as an Asian. I believe that.

Sokha, also from Cambodia, reports similar hostility occurring on an ongoing basis, particularly on public transport:

> Some white people look at me like I am an alien. When I take the bus, those people look at me in a discriminatory way. They stare at me from head to toe.

I expect that this type of discrimination against me and Asian people more broadly is increasing.

Buses or trains seem to be common sites for racist behaviour, as Sokha recounts:

I usually take the bus or train to work. Mostly people who commute in the same bus or train with me look at me in a disgusting way.

Beaches can also be a location for racist hostility, as observed by Hong, a Vietnamese worker:

When I went to the beach, a group of middle-aged ladies came to us and swore. They told us that us Asians should go back home. I just ignored them. I never suffer from discrimination because of religion and gender. It is all about racial discrimination.

Racism can occur anywhere, even outside schoolyards, as described in the following account from Seyha:

Some months ago, when I picked up my kids from school, I saw a man holding leaflets about something related to my skills (drug addiction and mental health). When I introduced myself, he said that there was no job for me there. I didn't even ask for a job. He was being discriminatory. I feel that wherever I go in Australia, I feel that I am discriminated against, mostly by Australian people.

Of course, inside the schoolyard racism can be even more prevalent, as described by Vichet:

Growing up in Australia, you will face racism. You will be told 'you are Asian'. It's easy for people to lash out at you if you are different from them. I got it a lot in high school from my fellow peers, the others. I was surprised. I felt anger. Those people are non-Asian. They are Europeans and they are Australians.

Higher education institutions are also not immune from racist behaviour, as described by Seyha:

There are certain issues at TAFE. The teacher treated me differently. If there are mistakes by the young Australian trainees, the teacher seems to treat those mistakes in a polite manner. But if it is my mistake, the teacher is not polite. She shouts at me. When I could not understand her words she said, 'You are killing me. You don't pay attention. I just explained everything!'

Some behaviours, while not overtly racist, have racial overtones, such as inappropriate questioning or over-effusive politeness. Seyha describes it in the following way:

She asked me how old I was and I said I am almost 40 years old. She looked surprised and said that I look young. She asked me what my husband was doing, and I said he is doing his PhD at the University of Queensland. She was again surprised. She asked me what I did back home, and I said I was a manager of a department. She was surprised. She also asked why I chose to study salon skills and I said because I cannot find the jobs related to my skills here. Somehow, she appeared discriminatory.

Other respondents such as Pheakdey describe being ignored and treated differently in their workplaces where, by law, they are meant to feel safe and respected:

> I used to encounter discrimination at work. I am a chef. I am Cambodian. I am short. I am not big enough. Most colleagues seem to look down on me. They seem to think that I cannot do the job properly. They don't tell me directly, but their behavior shows me that I am being discriminated against. I think those who discriminate against others are uneducated. Those who are highly educated don't discriminate against others.

Underlining the vulnerability of the Southeast Asian workers, the precariousness of their employment situation means that they are often new to their communities and in temporary and unsafe housing arrangements. The combined vulnerabilities can mean that they are often treated as outsiders who don't belong, with little recourse for corrective or legal action. There does not appear to be much that temporary workers can do to respond, other than to ignore it.

5.7 Bodily Health and Reproductive Choice

A significant concern, particularly for female temporary migrants from Southeast Asia, is that they are unable to plan to have children, especially when there is so much uncertainty around their visa status. This is a particular concern for women of reproductive age who sometimes have to wait for years before they have any certainty about their long-term visa status. Not being able to choose when to have a child translates into a broader sense of not having control over one's own personal environment and being able to plan for the future. Even though there is a focus on reproductive health in the UN's SDGs, with targets specifically focused on reproductive health in developing countries, there has been less focus on the barriers to reproductive decision-making for temporary migrants in developed countries. A component of SDG 5 ('Gender quality and women's empowerment'), for example, determines that women should be able to decide on their own sexual and reproductive health and rights. While Amartya Sen does not focus on reproductive health, having the choice to plan one's reproductive health can have a significant impact on human well-being.

Several Southeast Asian respondents were quite candid about this issue, with the uncertainty over visa and permanent residence status recurring themes. As Retno explains:

> To be honest, with this bridging visa and before I have an answer regarding my partner visa application, it somehow influences my life plan, too. For example, having a baby. I'm not sure if I can plan to have one in the future or not. I just want to wait until there's an answer regarding my partner visa. I don't want to be too confident to think that I will be granted a partner visa. There is of course still a possibility of it being rejected, so I need to be realistic about it.

Echoing this sentiment, an Indonesian migrant, Fitri, stated that 'I want to have children, but I don't think I would want to have a baby if my status is not clear yet'. Closely related to visa uncertainty, financial uncertainty also has an impact on reproductive decision-making. As described by Lia, one of the Indonesian respondents based in Perth, 'I don't want to suddenly have a baby, for example, without knowing how much money I will need each month to take care of him or her, how much money I will need for school, will we get a subsidy, and so on'. Childcare costs, especially for working families on a dual income, are often prohibitive. Trying to find a workaround for this can cause a great deal of inconvenience and hardship for temporary workers, as described by Lan, a Vietnamese migrant:

> I really want to send our fourth baby to childcare and start working but the childcare fees are so high. We do not receive any government subsidy for childcare. We cannot afford the fees. So, I still need to keep our baby at home. We do not receive any other government subsidy or support. During Covid, it was hard living and we needed to find a work around to survive.

The limits of childcare and education support can have the effect of shifting 'the cost of social reproduction from the state to the immigrants' (Bauder, 2006, p. 27). This, in turn, may increase migrants' dependence on employment, as well as wage theft and exploitation (Wright & Clibborn, 2020, p. 5). In other circumstances, without childcare, temporary migrants are unable to work at all and risk extreme poverty without having equal access to welfare assistance. Lia's reference to the pandemic here is salient. During the various waves of the pandemic in Australia, extended lockdowns of major cities such as Melbourne and Sydney as well as, to a lesser extent, Canberra, Brisbane, Adelaide and Perth had been accompanied by mass school and childcare closures. For a migrant worker couple, desperately trying to make ends meet working as taxi or Uber drivers, cleaners or abattoir workers without the opportunity for 'WFH' (Working from Home) arrangements or holding online meetings on their laptops from the comfort of their home offices, these lockdowns were incredibly difficult. For some couples, at least one of them, usually the mother, had to forgo or give up employment. As one Vietnamese woman observed, 'when the last kid grows up, I will seek a job'. In such a context, adding an extra child or two to an already stretched family unit has been, simply put, out of the question.

Not only are temporary migrant women unable to freely plan to have a child, but they are also less likely to have equal health outcomes if they end up having a child with a disability. In Australia, visas are granted to children with disabilities on the basis that the parents are granted visas on the proviso that they agree to cover the full costs associated with their child's disability, including medical care and additional expenses associated with special education. This can carry an enormous financial burden and affect the health and well-being of the whole family. Even worse, children with disabilities are usually rejected in Australia for permanent residency and citizenship, which is a risk that a temporary migrant would have to weigh up in having a child while on a temporary migrant visa.

6 Discussion

This research was informed by Amartya Sen and Martha Nussbaum's theoretical framework of capabilities (Sen, 2002, 2005; Nussbaum, 2011) and drew attention to the need for temporary migrants to be provided with at least a limited baseline set of social and political rights, as well as a degree of freedom and agency in their day-to-day life choices and planning. This is particularly important in the context of neoliberalism, where economic rights tend to supersede other social and political rights. Without a basic set of social and political rights, temporary migrants on low incomes often become victims of unscrupulous employers, unresponsive governments and occasionally partners who fail to look out for their welfare, especially in times of crisis.

In 2015, the United Nations adopted the SDGs, which are set to be achieved by the year 2030. Even though reducing inequality is a key part of the post-2015 development agenda, for as long as temporary migrants in developed countries lack a pathway to permanent residency and citizenship, their vulnerable circumstances are likely to remain subject to the dominant forces of neoliberal migration policies and agendas. For instance, while reducing poverty is a priority of the SDGs, a migration system that prioritises temporary migration over pathways to permanent residency hides the hidden pain, disempowerment and suffering of many temporary migrants in developed countries.

The findings in this research demonstrate the risks for temporary migrants in developed countries when the focus of the migration–development nexus is primarily on the economic contributions of migrants, in line with the neoliberal goals of governments. As demonstrated throughout this study, many of the migrants interviewed live in a state of 'liminal legality' (Torres & Wicks-Asburn, 2014; De Genova, 2002). While temporary migrants are clearly supporting the economy either as workers or as carers, they live in a never-ending state of bureaucratic and legal uncertainty waiting to hear back from the relevant government department on the outcome of their visa applications. The implications of this treatment on the health and social welfare of migrants are significant, as this study has revealed.

During the Covid-19 pandemic, in Australia migrants from Southeast Asia found themselves living in the depths of poverty without any welfare support and a limited capacity to return to their country of origin. As temporary migrants, many were classified as 'essential workers' by their employers, meaning that they were not able to work from home, and thus were more likely to contract the virus and pass it onto their families and friends. Situated in low-paid casualised and insecure work, and unable to assert their basic human rights out of fear that their employers or government authorities will cancel their visa, many felt that there was no one they could speak to in state or federal government agencies or departments. As non-citizens, they had been largely left to fend for themselves, except for ad hoc emergency cash or food packages provided by universities and local community groups.

A consistent theme throughout all the interviews conducted for this research was a lack of control over one's environment in terms of one's exposure to racism and discrimination, ability to plan for a family, to be employed in meaningful work, to live close to family and friends, and to have adequate health care. In other words, because of their temporary liminal resident status, they lack a wide variety of basic human rights such as having self-respect, being free to participate in society and being able to live a satisfying life in order to be able to fulfil their full capabilities such as having a fulfilling career, a family life and, most importantly, having a sense of dignity and belonging in society where they are treated with equality and respect. The combined impact is a widespread loss of opportunities and freedoms.

It is not unsurprising that temporary migrants find themselves in vulnerable circumstances given that, according to MIPEX, Australia lags behind other immigrant-receiving countries on indicators underpinning political rights, participation and integration. Without political rights and other avenues for political participation and integration, political parties at the state and federal level have little incentive to improve the circumstances of temporary migrants.

These migrants are, therefore, often doubly disenfranchised. This is because if they choose more informal modes of political participation such as protest and association, they may draw the unwelcome attention of government or law enforcement authorities – which, in the case of Australia's various Covid-19 lockdowns, may have included police officers and Australian Defence Force military personnel – as well as sponsoring employers, partners or other authorities in the shadow economy.

The experiences of temporary migrants discussed here and broadly experienced across Australia and other developed countries with similar migration schemes are unlikely to change unless there are pathways for permanent residency, citizenship, political rights and representation. As previously discussed, in the context of the Covid-19 pandemic there is now a real need to re-examine the existing development theories and policies to include political rights, membership and belonging so that countries are better prepared for future pandemics which are likely to further entrench social and political inequality unless action is taken.

There are implications for governments and civil society organisations if there are no changes at all to the existing temporary migration programmes in traditional settler countries such as Australia, the United States, Canada and New Zealand. Temporary migrants will continue to experience exploitation, poverty, violence, abuse, frustration and a lack of trust in the institutions that are meant to protect those in society who find themselves in vulnerable circumstances. Temporary migrants will continue to face discrimination, rejection, isolation and racism. As low-paid workers they are also more likely to be on the front line as victims of global pandemics, crime, rapid industrial change and environmental injustice. Women who find themselves in this situation may not be able to have children during their prime reproductive years. The likelihood of successful affective integration weakens as each year passes and more negative experiences become the norm, creating a trapdoor whereby migrants are stuck in a permanent temporary status with endless bureaucracy and unnecessary costs involving expensive medical check-ups of healthy adults and children in the prime of their life. In such a context with no changes afoot, governments will have failed to provide basic human rights, freedoms and agency – all necessary for temporary migrants to be able to make informed decisions about their future, and to contribute meaningfully to the societies and communities in which they reside.

The capabilities approach highlights an urgent task for governments to improve the quality of life for all people who reside within their country. The case studies of Southeast Asian migrants in this element reveal experiences not unlike those experienced in guest-worker systems previously practiced in

Western Europe, Singapore, Japan and in the Arab states of the Persian Gulf, and loudly shunned by the Australian government with its proud multicultural identity. However, Australia can ill-afford to rest its superior sense of pride on a multicultural identity that was established on a system of permanent migration, welfare assistance, good neighbourhood councils, anti-discrimination legislation, migrant resource centres, ethnic community councils, long-term job security, free education, strong trade unionism and labour protections.

The advance of neoliberalism in Australia, and the accompanying shift towards temporary skilled migration have wound back many protections that were once afforded to migrants brave enough to travel abroad for a better future for both themselves and their families. From a neoliberal perspective, the successes of multiculturalism can be found in the economic and social integration outcomes of Australia's second-generation migrants, whose parents often sacrificed fulfilling their own capabilities for their children's future. Australia gained from their sacrifices. However, Australia's identity as a successful multicultural country is compromised by its increasing emphasis on temporary skilled migration, which appears to be for economic expediency and political gain, with minimal political pain. Moreover, the social and political contributions of migrants have been de-emphasised in national discourse in favour of a neoliberal economic agenda that reduces migrants to an economic utility and ranked on a priority migration skilled occupation list.

If Australia is truly committed to multiculturalism, there are several policy changes that are recommended based on the experiences identified in this element. First, employer-sponsored visas restrict the freedom of movement and tie migrants to a place for a fixed amount of time. Under this program, migrants are unable to move freely between different employers. According to Horgan and Liinamaa (2017) this involves a form of 'social quarantining'. Collins observes that this can undermine social cohesion for citizens and non-citizens alike, as local authorities and communities are not incentivised to enhance their long-term inclusion (Collins, 2021, p. 193). Furthermore, and more concerningly, temporary migrants on employer-sponsored visas are vulnerable to exploitation and under-payment. In a review of temporary worker exploitation in New Zealand, a list of proposals was established to address exploitation in the industry such as introducing a labour hire licensing scheme which provides protections for workers, prohibiting people convicted of exploitation under the Immigration Act from managing a company, setting up a phone line for online reporting, developing a bridging visa for migrant workers who need to escape from an abusive situation and establishing immigration infringement offences for non-compliant employer behaviour that contributes to exploitation and vulnerability (New Zealand Ministry of Business,

Innovation and Employment, 2020). Temporary migrants on partner-sponsored visas may also find themselves vulnerable to mistreatment from their partner sponsor, as this element has outlined. This highlights the importance of providing information and emergency numbers to temporary migrants on partner visas about where to seek help in circumstances of domestic violence and coercive control. A bridging visa for migrants escaping violence is a necessity to ensure that migrants can exit from exploitative relationships.

Second, there is a need to improve the labour standards of temporary migrants to ensure that temporary migrants are provided with the same social and employment rights and entitlements as local citizens. Prior to 1996, migrant workers had comparable bargaining power and agency as Australian citizens, which prevented migrants from being exploited for their cheap labour (Wright & Clibborn, 2020). However, since then Australia's labour immigration laws, policies and regulations resemble those of a guest-worker regime, where migrants are unable to bargain for decent working conditions. Exacerbating the problem is the fact that migrants are frequently unable to move between employers, which limits the bargaining power of migrants to improve their working conditions. Temporary migrants in Australia are often denied many of the entitlements that citizens are entitled to, such as income protection in the event of workplace injury, and subsidised health care, education and unemployment benefits (Wright & Clibborn, 2020). Australia needs to strengthen institutional protections so that there is not a differential treatment between temporary migrants and permanent residents and citizens.

Third, there needs to be a limited time of temporariness. The experiences of temporary migrants discussed in this element reveal a pattern of utilising bridging visas to transition from one temporary visa subclass to another temporary visa subclass, with the hope of being offered a permanent visa. The long-term temporary status of migrants beyond five years increases the time period that migrants are excluded from the democratic polity. The longer that migrants are in a state of liminality, the longer they are excluded as second-class citizens and from the democratic polity (see Mares, 2017, p. 10). This is inconsistent with the traditional values of a liberal democracy. According to Carens (2008, p. 419), 'the inner logic of democracy and a commitment to liberal principles require the full inclusion of the entire settled population'. If we are to take the liberal values of equality and freedom seriously, Australia could begin with a debate on the extension of the franchise to non-citizen permanent residents, following in the footsteps of New Zealand. This requires developing a national conversation or debate on electoral and citizenship reforms to demonstrate a genuine commitment to the value of diversity and inclusion.

Fourth, the skill threshold is one way of measuring the value of temporary migrants and whether they should be allowed entry into Australia. However, if we reflect on the successful history of permanent migration and settlement in Australia, there are many other contributions and opportunities that are lost in the focus on skills and economic contributions. Migrants contribute far more to society than their mere skills, education and employment experience. Other priorities could be considered during their time as temporary migrants that have unique social value, such as volunteer work, coaching a sports team, caring for a person with disabilities, leading an organisation or social movement, joining a political party, joining a community club or interest group, or winning a prestigious award. These are just a few of the thousands of contributions that temporary migrants make which add social value to society. There are also broader ethical questions in the migration–development nexus about social value. Does a child with a disability not add value to Australian society? In Australia, the Migration Act allows families who are not permanent residents to be deported if their children have a disability. I would argue that as a compassionate society, children with disabilities should be welcomed, as they bring joy, love and happiness to their family and friends. They have unique value which cannot be empirically measured through a skills test that can only measure human worth on a productivity scale.

Fifth, building a national debate in politics depends on having voices in politics that are sympathetic to the concerns of temporary migrants. This involves strengthening the organising capacity of temporary migrants to have their voices heard within the electorate. This cannot be achieved if temporary migrants are isolated and threatened with deportation if they do not meet the strict requirements of their visa that binds them to a place, a person or an employer. Ensuring that there are opportunities for social and political advocacy empowers temporary migrants to change their circumstances for the better through advocating for electoral and citizenship reforms. Temporary migrants need freedom of movement and freedom of speech, without fear of deportation so that they can mobilise community and political representatives to take up their cause. Politicians will also be incentivised to better respond to the interests and experiences of new migrants if there is a likelihood of public hostility following reports of exploitation. An independent study has found that more than 80 per cent of Australians support pathways to permanent residency (HRLC, 2021). This is supported by a longer-term trend that Australians have favourable attitudes towards migration in general (Cameron & McAllister, 2019). However, Australians are deeply unhappy with the exploitative nature of temporary migration. Temporary migrants need to be given opportunities to be heard rather than silenced, in order to mobilise public sentiment in their favour.

Finally, at a global level we need to radically rethink the idea of 'long-term' temporary migration as a successful economic model for sending and receiving countries. Within migration studies, temporary migrants are frequently viewed as a mobile economic resource for development at local, national and international levels. As countries compete for highly skilled and cheap labour, there appears to be few global or regional norms established to ensure temporary migrants are protected with the necessary social, economic and political rights to fully realise their capabilities. With the notable exceptions of socially progressive countries like New Zealand, few immigrant-receiving countries are prepared to allow temporary migrants to be enfranchised as non-citizen residents and provided with a pathway to citizenship and the political rights associated with it. For this reason, international pressure should be applied on nation states to agree to a common set of principles and guidelines that focus not only on economic development but also on the development of human capabilities, thus enhancing the capacity of migrants to realise their full potential as equal members of the *demos*.

References

Adkins, L., Cooper, M. & Konings, M. (2019). Class in the 21st century: Asset inflation and the new logic of inequality. *Environment and Planning A: Economy and Space*, **53**(3), 548–572.

Agunias, D. R. & Newland, K. (2007). *Circular Migration and Development: Trends, Policy Routes and Ways Forward*, Washington, DC: Migration Policy Institute.

Allerton, C. (2017). Contested statelessness in Sabah, Malaysia: Irregularity and the politics of recognition. *Journal of Immigrant and Refugee Studies*, **15** (3), 250–268.

Anand, P., Hunter, G. Carter, I & Dowding, K. (2009). The development of capability indicators. *Journal of Human Development and Capabilities*, **10** (1), 125–152.

Anderson, B. (2010). Migration, immigration controls and the fashioning of precarious workers. *Work, Employment and Society*, **24**(2), 300–317.

Arrighi, J. T. & Bauböck, R. (2017). A multilevel puzzle: Migrants' voting rights in national and local elections. *European Journal of Political Research*, **56**, 619–639.

Australian Associated Press (AAP) (2021). Anne Aly says Labor's move to parachute Kristina Keneally into Fowler is a 'huge failure' on diversity. *Guardian Australia*. www.theguardian.com/australia-news/2021/sep/11/anne-aly-says-labors-move-to-parachute-kristina-keneally-into-fowler-is-a-huge-failure-on-diversity

Australian Bureau of Statistics (ABS) (2017a). Census TableBuilder. Canberra: Australian Government. www.abs.gov.au/websitedbs/censushome.nsf/home/tablebuilder

Australian Bureau of Statistics (ABS) (2017b). Cultural Diversity in Australia. Canberra: Australian Government. www.abs.gov.au/ausstats/abs@.nsf/Lookup/by%20Subject/2071.0~2016~Main%20Features~Cultural%20Diversity%20Data%20Summary~30

Australian Bureau of Statistics. (2019). Characteristics of Recent Migrants, Australia. Canberra: Australian Government. https://www.abs.gov.au/statistics/people/people-and-communities/characteristics-recent-migrants/latest-release#:~:text=At%20November%202019%2C%209.1%25%20of,(Table%201)

Australian Bureau of Statistics. (2021). Migration, Australia. Canberra: Australian Government. www.abs.gov.au/statistics/people/population/migration-australia/latest-release

Australian Department of Home Affairs. (2022). Visa Processing Times. Canberra: Australian Government. https://immi.homeaffairs.gov.au/visas/getting-a-visa/visa-processing-times/family-visa-processing-priorities/parent-visas-queue-release-dates

Australian Election Study (AES) (1993). *Australian Election Study*. Canberra: Australian Data Archives.

Australian Election Study (AES) (1996). *Australian Election Study*. Canberra: Australian Data Archives.

Australian Government Department of Home Affairs (2022). Visa Processing Times. Canberra: Australian Government. https://immi.homeaffairs.gov.au/visas/getting-a-visa/visa-processing-times/global-visa-processing-times

Barker, F. & McMillan, K. (2016). Access to Electoral Rights. New Zealand: European University Institute, Florence Robert Schuman Centre for Advanced Studies EUDO Citizenship Observatory. http://eudo-citizenship.eu

Baubock, R. (2007). Stakeholder citizenship and transnational political participation: A normative evaluation of external voting. *Fordham Law Review*, **75** (5), 2394–2447.

Bauböck, R. (2015). Morphing the demos into the right shape: Normative principles for enfranchising resident aliens and expatriate citizens. *Democratization*, **22**(5), 820–839.

Bauder, H. (2006). *Labor Movement: How Migration Regulates Labor Markets*, New York: Oxford University Press.

Bellamy, R. (2007). *Political Constitutionalism: A Republican Defence of the Constitutionality of Democracy*, Cambridge: Cambridge University Press.

Benton, M. (2010). The tyranny of the enfranchised majority? The accountability of states to their non-citizen population. *Res Publica*, **16**(4), 397–413.

Benton, M. (2014). The problem of denizenship: A non-domination framework. *International Social and Political Philosophy*, **17**(1), 49–69.

Blainey, G. (1984). *All For Australia*, Melbourne: Methuen.

Boucher, A. (2020). How 'skill' definition affects the diversity of skilled immigration policies. *Journal of Ethnic and Migration Studies*, **46**(12), 2533–2550.

Boucher, A. & Gest, J. (2018). *Crossroads: Comparative Immigration Regimes in a World of Demographic Change*, Cambridge: Cambridge University Press.

Boucher, A. & Pacquet, M. (2021). *The Politics of Immigration Backlogs*, Paper presented at the Australian Political Science Association conference, Macquarie University, 20 September 2021.

Briones, L. (2011). Rights with capabilities: Towards a social justice framework for migrant activism. *Studies in Social Justice*, **5**(1), 127–143.

Butterworth, L. (2021). COVID-19 lockdown exposes feelings of 'two cities' emerging within Sydney, Q+A hears. *ABC News*. www.abc.net.au/news/2021-09-17/q-a-wrap-sydney-two-cities-emerging/100469236

Cameron, S. & McAllister, I. (2019). Trends in Australian Political Opinion: Results from the Australian Election Study. https://australianelectionstudy.org/wp-content/uploads/Trends-in-Australian-Political-Opinion-1987-2019.pdf

Carens, J. (2014). An overview of the ethics of immigration. *Critical Review of International Social and Political Philosophy*, **17**(5), 538–559.

Carens, J. (2008). Live-in domestics, seasonal workers, and others hard to locate on the map of democracy. *Journal of Political Philosophy*, **16**(4), 419–455.

Carney, T. (2007). Reforming social security: Improving incentives and capabilities. *Griffith Law Review*, **16**(1), 1–26.

Castles, S. (1992). The Australian model of immigration and multiculturalism: Is it applicable to Europe. *The International Migration Review*, **26**(2), 549–567.

Clibborn, S. & Wright, C. (2018). Employer theft of temporary migrant workers' wages in Australia: Why has the state failed to act? *Economics and Labour Relations Review*, **29**(2), 207–227.

Coates, B., Sherrell, H. & Mackey, W. (2022). Fixing Temporary Skilled Migration. Grattan Institute. https://grattan.edu.au/report/fixing-temporary-skilled-migration/

Collins, F. (2021). Temporary migration and regional development amidst Covid-19: Invercargill and Queenstown. *New Zealand Geographer*, **77**(3), 191–205.

Cooke, F., & Mulia, D. S. (2012). Migration and moral panic: The case of oil palm in Sabah, East Malaysia. In O.Pye, ed., *The Transnationalism of Oil Palm*, Singapore: Institute of Southeast Asian Studies, pp. 140–163.

Cornwell, A. & Brock, K. (2005). What do buzzwords do for development policy? A critical look at 'participation', 'empowerment' and 'poverty reduction'. *Third World Quarterly*, **26**(7), 1043–1060.

Dalton, R., Farrell, D. & McAllister, I. (2011). *Political Parties and Democratic Linkage: How Parties Organize Democracy*, New York: Oxford University Press.

Davey, M. (2021). What went wrong: How delta exposed the NSW approach to Covid. *Guardian Australia*. www.theguardian.com/australia-news/2021/jul/10/what-went-wrong-how-delta-exposed-the-nsw-approach-to-covid

Davies, S. (2019). *Containing Contagion: the Politics of Disease Outbreaks in Southeast Asia*, Baltimore: John Hopkins University Press.

de Haas, H. (2012). The migration and development pendulum: A critical view on research and policy. *International Migration*, **50**(3), 8–25.

De Genova, N. (2002). Migrant 'illegality' and deportability in everyday life. *Annual Review of Anthropology*, **31**(1), 419–47.

Department of Home Affairs. (2021). New Regional Visas. https://immi.home affairs.gov.au/visas/working-in-australia/regional-migration/regional-visas

Dustmann, C. & Preston, I. (2007). Racial and economic factors in attitudes to immigration. *The B.E. Journal of Economic Analysis & Policy*, **7**(1), 1–39.

Ernest, D. C. (2015). The enfranchisement of resident aliens: Variations and explanations. *Democratization*, **22**(5), 861–883.

Facchini, G. & Mayda, A. M. (2006). Individual attitudes towards immigrants: Welfare-state determinants across countries, *CReAM Discussion Paper No 04/06*. London: Centre for Research and Analysis of Migration, Department of Economics, Drayton House, 1–34.

Farbotko, C. & Lazrus, H. (2012). The first climate refugees? Contesting global narratives of climate change in Tuvalu. *Global Environmental Change*, **22**(2), 382–390.

Frank, S. (2006). Project Mahathir: 'Extraordinary' population growth in Sabah. *Südostasien aktuell: Journal of Current Southeast Asian Affairs*, **25**(5), 71–80.

Freeman, G. (2006). Politics and mass immigration. In R. Goodin and C. Tilly, eds., *The Oxford Handbook of Contextual Political Analysis*, Oxford: Oxford University Press, pp. 636–648.

Guadagno, L. (2020). MRS No. 60 – Migrants and the COVID-19 Pandemic: An Initial Analysis, in Migration Research Series/Users/s2989370/Downloads/mrs-60.pdf.

Guan, Q. & Pietsch, J. (2022). The impact of intergroup contact on attitudes towards immigrants: A case study of Australia. *Ethnic and Racial Studies*, https://doi.org/10.1080/01419870.2021.2007277. This article will be published in ERS Volume 45 Issue 12, but page numbers are not yet available until October 2022.

Haas, H. D., Castles, S. & Miller, M. (2019). *The Age of Migration: Sixth Edition*, London: Macmillan International.

Hahamovitch, C. (2003). Creating perfect immigrants: Guestworkers of the world in historical perspective. *Labour History*, **44**(1), 69–94.

Hammar, T. (1990). *Democracy and the Nation-State: Aliens, Denizens, and Citizens in a World of International Migration*: Aldershot, Hants, England: Avebury; Brookfield, Vt.: Gower Pub. Co.

Hartwich, O. M. (2011). Selection, Migration and Integration: Why Multiculturalism Works in Australia (And Fails in Europe). *CIS Policy Mongoraphy* 121.

Haydar, N. (2021). MP Anne Aly slams Labor 'hypocrisy' over plan to parachute Kristina Keneally into multicultural Fowler. *ABC News*. www.abc.net.au/news/2021-09-11/anne-aly-criticises-labor-diversity-kristina-keneally-fowler/100454412

Horgan, M. & Liinamaa, S. (2017). The social quarantining of migrant labour: Everyday effects of temporary foreign worker regulation in Canada. *Journal of Ethnic and Migration Studies*, **43**(5), 713–730.

Howe, J., Charlesworth, S. & Brennan, D. (2019). Migration pathways for frontline care workers in Australia and New Zealand: Front doors, side doors, back doors and trap doors. *University of New South Wales Law Journal*, **42**(1), 2011–241.

Hugo, G. (2008). Immigrant settlement outside of Australia's capital cities. *Population, Space and Place*, **14**, 553–571.

Hugo, G., Wall, J. & Young, M. (2015). *The Southeast Asia-Australia Regional Migration System: Some Insights into the 'New Emigration'*, Washington, DC: Migration Policy Institute.

Human Rights Law Centre (HRLC). (2021). The Essential Report. Essential Research. www.hrlc.org.au/news/2022/2/1/australians-overwhelmingly-support-permanent-residency-for-migrants

Institute for Democracy and Electoral Assistance (IDEA) (2018). Political Participation of Refugees: Bridging the Gaps. Stockholm, Sweden, International IDEA.

International Labour Organisation (ILO) (2021). Labour Migration and Migrant Workers in the 2030 Agenda for Sustainable Development. www.ilo.org

International Organisation for Migration (IOM) (2020). International Strategy on Migration and Sustainable Development. https://publications.iom.int

Isin, E. F. (2002). *Being Political: Genealogies of Citizenship*, Minnesota: University of Minnesota Press.

Jupp, J. (1995). From 'white Australia' to 'part of Asia': Recent shifts in Australian immigration policy towards the region. *International Migration Review*, **29**(1), 207–208.

Jupp, J. & Pietsch, J. (2018). Migrant and ethnic politics in the 2016 election. In A. Gauja, P. Chen, J. Curtin and J. Pietsch, eds., *Double Disillusion: The 2016 Australian Federal Election*, Canberra: ANU Press, pp. 661–679.

Karp, P. and Remeikis, A. (2021). Kristina Keneally confirms bid for western Sydney seat as critics accuse Labor of sacrificing diversity. *Guardian Australia*. www.theguardian.com/australia-news/2021/sep/10/kristina-keneallys-bid-for-lower-house-seat-of-fowler-a-missed-opportunity-labor-critics-say

Kim, C. K. (2005). Asian American Employment in the Federal Civil Service. *Public Administration Quarterly*, **28**(4), 430–459.

Kluge, H. H. P., Jakab, Z., Bartovic, J., D'Anna, V. & Severoni, S. (2020). Refugee and migrant health in the COVID-19 response. *The Lancet* **395** (10232) Volume 395, 1237–1239.

Kontominas, B. & Taouk, M. (2021). NSW police deny targeting multicultural communities in Covid-19 operation. *ABC News*. www.abc.net.au/news/ 2021-07-09/nsw-police-defend-COVID-19-operation-in-south-west-syd ney/100280106

Kwok, J. T. & Pietsch, J. (2017). The political representation of Asian-Australian populations since the end of white Australia, *AAPI Nexus Journal: Policy, Practice and Community*, UCLA: Asian American Studies Center (Fall Edition).

Lichter, D. T., Johnson, K. M. Turner, R. N. & Churilla, A. (2012). Hispanic assimilation and fertility in new U.S. destinations. *International Migration Review*, **46**(4), 767–791.

López-Guerra, C. (2005). Should expatriates vote? *Journal of Political Philosophy*, **13**(2), 216–234.

Lui, I., Vandan, N., Davies, S. et al. (2021). We deserve help during the pandemic: The effect of the COVID-19 pandemic on foreign domestic workers in Hong Kong. *Journal of Migration and Health*, 3 (volume 3, **DOI** https://doi.org/10.1016/j.jmh.2021.100037 The website is https:// www.sciencedirect.com/science/article/pii/S2666623521000040, 100037).

Mares, P. (2012). Temporary Migration and its Implications for Australia. Papers on Parliament No. 57. www.aph.gov.au/About_Parliament/Senate/ Powers_practice_n_procedures/pops/pop57/c03

Mares, P. (2017). Locating temporary migrants on the map of Australian democracy. *Migration, Mobility, & Displacement*, **3**(1), 9–31.

McAllister, I. & Ravenhill, J. (1998). Australian attitudes towards closer engagement with Asia. *Pacific Review*, **11**(1), 119–141.

McMillan, K. (2017). 'Affective integration' and access to the rights of permanent residency: New Zealanders resident in Australia post-2001. *Ethnicities*, **17**(1), 103–127.

Migration Policy Group. (2021). Migration Integration Policy Index. www .migpolgroup.com/_old/diversity-integration/migrant-integration-policy-index/.

Missbach, A. (2015). Transiting asylum seekers in Indonesia: Between human rights protection and criminalisation. In J. Pietsch & M. Clark, eds., *Migration and integration in Europe, Southeast Asia, and Australia*, Amsterdam: Amsterdam University Press, pp. 115–135.

Missbach, A. (2018). Citizenship elegy: In search of the elusive passport. *Griffith Review*, **61**, 38–42.

Morales, L. (2009). *Joining Political Institutions: Institutions, Mobilisation and Participation in Western Democracies*, Colchester: ECPR Press.

Naudé, W., Santos-Paulino, A. & Mcgillivray, M. (2009). Measuring vulnerability: An overview and introduction. *Oxford Development Studies*, **37**(3), 183–191.

New Zealand Ministry of Business, Innovation & Employment. (2020). The Temporary Migrant Worker Exploitation Review: A Summary of Proposals, New Zealand Government. www.mbie.govt.nz/dmsdocument/11801-temporary-migrant-worker-exploitation-review-final-proposals-proactiverelease-pdf

Nussbaum, M. (2011). *Creating Capabilities: The Human Development Approach*, Cambridge, MA: Harvard University Press.

Nussbaum, M. (2019). *The Cosmopolitan Tradition: A Noble but Flawed Ideal*, Harvard: Harvard University Press.

Organisation for Economic Co-operation and Development (OECD) (2019). International Migration Outlook Report. www.oecd-ilibrary.org

Owen, D. (2012). Constituting the polity, constituting the demos: On the place of the all affected interests principle in democratic theory and in resolving the democratic boundary problem. *Ethics and Global Politics*, **5**(3), 129–152.

Pedroza, L. (2014). The democratic potential of enfranchising resident migrants. *International Migration*, **53**(3), 22–35.

Pettigrew, T. & Tropp, L. (2006). A meta-analytic test of intergroup contact theory. *Journal of Personality and Social Psychology*, **90**(5), 751–783.

Pettigrew, T. & Tropp, L. (2011). *When Groups Meet: The Dynamics of Intergroup Contact*. New York: Psychology Press.

Pfister, T. (2012). Citizenship and capability? Amartya Sen's capabilities approach from a citizenship perspective. *Citizenship Studies*, **16**(2), 241–254.

Pietsch, J. (2017a). Explaining the political under-representation of Asian Australians: Geographical concentration and voting patterns. *Political Science*, **69**(2), 161–174.

Pietsch, J. (2017b). Diverse outcomes: Social citizenship and the inclusion of skilled immigrants in Australia. *Social Inclusion*, **5**(1), 32–44.

Pietsch, J. (2018). *Race, Ethnicity and the Participation Gap: Understanding Australia's Political Complexion*, Toronto: University of Toronto Press.

Pietsch, J. (2020). Australian ethnic change and political inclusion: Finding strength in diversity in responding to global crises. In S. Saggar. Ed. *Reimagining Australia: Migration, Culture, Diversity*. Perth: University of Western Australia Press.

Plewa, P. (2007). The rise and fall of temporary foreign worker policies: Lessons for Poland. *International Migration*, **45**(2), 3–36.

Preibisch, K. Dodd, W. & Su, Y. (2016). Pursuing the capabilities approach within the migration–development nexus. *Journal of Ethnic and Migration Studies*, **42**(13), 2111–2127.

Ramia, G. Mitchell, E. Morris, A. Hastings, C. & Wilson, S. (2021). Explaining Policy Inaction on Student International Housing, Paper presented as the Australian Political Science Association conference, Macquarie University, 20 September 2021.

Regional Australia Institute (RAI) (2018). Population Dynamics in Regional Australia. www.regionalaustralia.org.au

Remeikis, A. (2021). Does federal parliament accurately reflect the evolving face of diverse Australia? *Guardian Australia.* www.theguardian.com/australia-news/2021/sep/18/does-federal-parliament-accurately-reflect-the-evolving-face-of-diverse-australia?CMP=Share_AndroidApp_Other

Robeyns, I. (2006). The capability approach in practice. *Journal of Political Philosophy*, **14**(3), 351–376.

Sadiq, K. (2005). When states prefer non-citizens over citizens: Conflict over illegal immigration into Malaysia. *International Studies Quarterly*, **49**(1), 101–122.

Saith, A. (2006). From universal values to millennium development goals: Lost in translation. *Development and Change*, **37**(6), 1167–1199.

Sayer, A. (2012). Capabilities, contributive injustice and unequal divisions of labour. *Journal of Human Development*, **13**(4), 580–596.

Scheve, K. & Slaughter, M. (2001b). Labour market competition and individual preferences over immigration policy. *Review of Economics and Statistics*, **83**(1), 133–145.

Sen, A. (1985). *Commodities and Capabilities*, Amsterdam: North-Holland.

Sen, A. (1999). *Development as Freedom*, Oxford: Oxford University Press.

Sen, A. (2002). *Rationality and Freedom*, Cambridge, MA: Harvard University Press.

Sen, A. (2005). Human rights and capabilities. *Journal of Human Development*, **6**(2), 151–166.

Sen, A. (2009). *The Idea of Justice*, London: Allen Lane.

Sen, A. & Williams, B. (1982). *Utilitarianism and Beyond*, Cambridge: Cambridge University Press.

Simons, M. (2020). Melbourne Towers' sudden hard lockdown caught police, health workers and residents off-guard. *Guardian Australia.* www.theguardian.com/australia-news/2021/jul/04/we-thought-we-were-australian-melbourne-tower-lockdown-lives-on-in-legacy-of-trauma

Simons, M. (2021). We thought we were Australian: Melbourne Tower lockdown lives on in legacy of trauma. *Guardian Australia*. www.theguardian.com/australia-news/2021/jul/04/we-thought-we-were-australian-melbourne-tower-lockdown-lives-on-in-legacy-of-trauma

Stringer, C. & Michailova, S. (2019). Understanding the Exploitation of Temporary Migrant Workers: A Comparison of Australia, Canada, New Zealand and the United Kingdom. New Zealand Ministry of Business, Innovation and Employment. www.mbie.govt.nz/dmsdocument/7110-understanding-the-exploitation-of-temporary-migrant-workers-a-comparison-of-australia-canada-new-zealand-and-the-united-kingdom

Thompson, A. (2022). Delivery rider deaths could be subject of coronial inquest. *The Sydney Morning Herald*. www.smh.com.au/national/nsw/delivery-rider-deaths-could-be-subject-of-coronial-inquest-20220228-p5a0al.html

Torres, R. M. & Wicks-Asburn, M. (2014). Undocumented students' narratives of liminal citizenship: High aspirations, exclusion, and "in-between" identities. *Professional Geographer*, **66**(2), 195–204.

United Nations Development Programme (UNDP) (2020). The Next Frontier: Human Development and the Anthropocene. *UNDP Human Development Report 2020*, New York, USA: UNDP.

United Nations Human Rights Council (UNHRC) (2010). Report on the Independent Expert of Minority Issues, Gay McDougall. https://documents-dds-ny.un.org/doc/UNDOC/GEN/G10/101/98/PDF/G1010198.pdf?OpenElement

Vasta, E. (2004). Community, the state and the deserving citizen: Pacific Islanders in Australia. *Journal of Ethnic and Migration Studies*, **30**(1), 195–213.

Victorian Ombudsman (2020). Investigation into the Detention and Treatment of Public Housing Residents Arising From a COVID-19 'Hard Lockdown' in July 2020. https://assets.ombudsman.vic.gov.au/assets/Reports/Parliamentary-Reports/Public-housing-tower-lockdown/Victorian-Ombudsman-report-Investigation-into-the-detention-and-treatment-of-public-housing-residents-arising-from-a-COVID-19-hard-lockdown-in-July-2020.pdf?mtime=20201216075340

Wolff, J. & De-Shalit, A. (2007). *Disadvantage*, Oxford: Oxford University Press.

Worthington, M. (2021). Labor's Fowler parachute for Kristina Keneally leaves a succession plan in tatters and a diversity problem. *ABC News*. www.abc.net.au/news/2021-09-12/kristina-keneally-fowler-labor-diversity-woes-tu-le/100451344

Wright, C. & Clibborn, S. (2020). A guest-worker state? The declining power and agency of migrant labour in Australia. *Economics and Labour Relations Review*, **31**(1), 34–58.

Acknowledgements

I wish to thank Nadia Farabi, Thu Nguyen and Sovinda Po for their valuable research insights and contributions to this Element, specifically in relation to assistance with fieldwork interviews and translation. I would also like to express my deepest appreciation to the anonymous participants for their valuable time and openness in sharing what can sometimes be very heartbreaking and broken life journeys. I would like to thank the Centre for Governance and Public Policy at Griffith University and the Director Kai He for providing the research funds and support for the Element. I am very grateful to the Series Editor Peter Ho for his inspiration and to the anonymous reviewers who provided me with excellent feedback from their own expertise to improve my earlier drafts. Special thanks to my colleagues Qing Guan, James Raymer, Anna Boucher, Terry Carney, Reyvi Marinas, Antje Missbach, Susan Kneebone, Susan Harris Rimmer, Sara Davies, Robert Hales and Andreas Chai for interdisciplinary research collaborations on temporary migration and population movements across the region and for sharing ideas and expertise throughout the time of this Element. Finally, I would like to thank my beautiful family Marshall, Peter, Tristan and Alina.

Cambridge Elements ☰

Global Development Studies

Peter Ho
Zhejiang University

Peter Ho is Distinguished Professor at Zhejiang University and high-level National Expert of China. He has held or holds the position of, amongst others, Research Professor at the London School of Economics and Political Science and the School of Oriental and African Studies, Full Professor at Leiden University and Director of the Modern East Asia Research Centre, Full Professor at Groningen University and Director of the Centre for Development Studies. Ho is well-cited and published in leading journals of development, planning and area studies. He published numerous books, including with Cambridge University Press, Oxford University Press, and Wiley-Blackwell. Ho achieved the William Kapp Prize, China Rural Development Award, and European Research Council Consolidator Grant. He chairs the International Conference on Agriculture and Rural Development (www.icardc.org) and sits on the boards of *Land Use Policy*, *Conservation and Society*, *China Rural Economics*, *Journal of Peasant Studies*, and other journals.

Servaas Storm
Delft University of Technology

Servaas Storm is a Dutch economist who has published widely on issues of macroeconomics, development, income distribution & economic growth, finance, and climate change. He is a Senior Lecturer at Delft University of Technology. He obtained a PhD in Economics (in 1992) from Erasmus University Rotterdam and worked as consultant for the ILO and UNCTAD. His latest book, co-authored with C.W.M. Naastepad, is *Macroeconomics Beyond the NAIRU* (Harvard University Press, 2012) and was awarded with the 2013 Myrdal Prize of the European Association for Evolutionary Political Economy. Servaas Storm is one of the editors of *Development and Change* (2006-now) and a member of the Institute for New Economic Thinking's Working Group on the Political Economy of Distribution.

Advisory Board
Arun Agrawal, *University of Michigan*
Jun Borras, *International Institute of Social Studies*
Daniel Bromley, *University of Wisconsin-Madison*
Jane Carruthers, *University of South Africa*
You-tien Hsing, *University of California, Berkeley*
Tamara Jacka, *Australian National University*

About the Series
The Cambridge Elements on Global Development Studies publishes ground-breaking, novel works that move beyond existing theories and methodologies of development in order to consider social change in real times and real spaces.

Cambridge Elements ≡

Global Development Studies

Elements in the Series

Temporary Migrants from Southeast Asia in Australia: Lost Opportunities
Juliet Pietsch

A full series listing is available at: www.cambridge.org/EGDS